the Sins of Kalamazoo
The Unsolved Murder of Louis Schilling, and the Crimes That Shaped a Community

J. Thomas Buttery

Dedicated to Anne, Maxwell, Lincoln, and Harrison

Nestled in southwest Michigan nearly equidistant from
Chicago & Detroit the City of Kalamazoo is the county seat
of Kalamazoo County. *The Columbian World's Fair Atlas pg. 102.*
H. Stiles' Sons & Co, Warren, OH. 1893

Contents

Preface

THE FOLLOWING IS both an account of the Louis Schilling murder case and a contextual exploration of significant Kalamazoo crimes throughout the 19th and early 20th centuries. Anecdotes, as well as the "scrap book" of William S. Downey's law enforcement career, have been included in the hopes that a firm understanding of the setting and period during which the Schilling murder occurred can be reached by the reader. In an effort to provide the best possible understanding of how all of the offenses contained within this book occurred, why some went unsolved, and their significance in Kalamazoo's history I have limited the inclusion of speculative story-telling in favor of fact-based writing. As a result nearly every detail or event described within this book has been gleaned from original sources, the majority of which were period specific newspaper articles. As you may notice as you read the numerous quotes found within this book the journalists of the day wrote with a certain level of panache not often found in contemporary journalism. In an attempt to replicate this style of writing I have incorporated some of the period flamboyance and verbiage into my work. In addition to the unique writing style of the day, journalism of this period leaned heavily towards sensationalism, while often maintaining a tentative grasp on the facts. I have made every attempt to omit claims, insinuations, and details that I know to be false. In other instances where news accounts were fantastical and their truthfulness questionable I have attempted to make that clear. The same holds true for the personalities found in this work. Within are a number of individuals that may come across as heroes, villains, or otherwise. I did not choose their position in this story, but rather I have simply guided the narrative established by their contemporaries. The last thing I would like to address is the issue of "solving" the Schilling murder. In keeping with my effort to limit speculation you will not find a decisive verdict regarding the identity of the murderer within this book. Instead, I have provided all of the pertinent facts as I see them, and you are free to draw conclusions as to the likely murderer. And while I do not definitively proclaim my verdict regarding the identity of the murderer, I do believe he can be found within these pages.

Acknowledgements

I WOULD LIKE to thank my wife, sons, parents, extended family, and friends for their support. I would also like to thank a number of local organizations and the hard-working people who have assisted me during my research: The Kalamazoo Valley Museum, the Kalamazoo Public Library, the Zhang Legacy Collections Center at Western Michigan University, the Grand Rapids Public Museum, and the North Berrien Historical Museum.

Citizens of Kalamazoo engage in intellectual pursuits
at the city's newly opened public library c1893.
From the collection of the Kalamazoo Public Library

Introduction

"So far refined that in all my walks through town, I have not heard language by men or boys which is not fit to be used around any family hearth, and have wondered whether such refinement was owing to the taste so universally displayed here in architecture, landscape, gardening, and in every ambitious and expensive method of beautifying homes and their surroundings." Vital Emanuel Bangs - California State Assemblyman and former resident of Kalamazoo.

Stanislaus (Cal) News, August 10, 1883

WHILE SOME MAY laugh at the name, I assure you, friend, that Kalamazoo is an indisputably serious community, having reached its current state of justifiable notoriety through solemn trials and powerful tribulation. For, as you may well know, great men and women are not formed in the tepid waters of comfort and leisure; it is here in the untamed forests, harsh winters, and furrowed streets of the Midwest that the forge of destiny lies ready to shape the powerful individuals who desire to call this place home. Largely defiant in the face of such adversity, our forebears built a community unique in its success but common in its faults. As culture forms and enterprise blossoms in the heartland of America it does so in a communal soil that also yields a healthy

1

crop of ignorance, greed, and immorality. Often forgotten, instances of rebellious unproductivity have frequently stained the pages of our collective history. No one such moment has imprinted itself on the consciousness of this community so deeply as the foul act that befell respected butcher Louis Schilling. Unanswered and unavenged his murder stands out as an unusually rotten act in an otherwise cultivated city. Less recollected are the numerous contemptible deeds of many a desperate man and those who sought to curb their destructive undertakings. William S. Downey is one such individual, whose life was principally spent calmly maintaining order while at work in the field of law, plucking unsavory weeds from fertile Midwest ground. Intertwined and reflective in both their success and tragedy, the lives of Louis Schilling and William S. Downey cannot be separated from one another any more than the following misdeeds can be separated from the annals of Kalamazoo history.[1]

---

1 *The placard above the Schilling Market read "Lewis Schilling", in this text he is referred to as Louis. Mr. Schilling's given name was in fact Louis, but it appears he took to using what he may have considered to be the more American version of the name sometime after 1870. As he was most commonly referred to as "Louis" in the papers it will be the version of his name used in this text.*

The Committee of police offered a resolution that the council proceed to ballot for six policeman and that the salary of said policemen be fixed at $50 per month each.

Whole number of votes...11

Wm. Downey............................9

John Gordon.........................1

Wm. Hare..................................1

Mr. Downey was declared elected

April 24, 1885

Officers Downey and Dustin were summoned to the "dock" last evening to quell an incipient riot. Messrs. George and John Glover arrived just in time to see the disturbance quieted; and being struck with remorse at not having arrived in time to see the fun they proceeded to stir up a little riot on their own hook. One struck Downey a stinging and unexpected blow in the face. The other belted Dustin, who was taken unawares, across the cheek and turned to run. Downey gathered his assailant in without much difficulty, and Dustin captured his after a chase of two blocks. The interesting pair were marched triumphantly to the courthouse square and given lodgings in the county jail.

June 12, 1885

Policeman Downey run in a boy today with some characteristics of John L. Sullivan - he was drunk, full of wind and on his muscle. If the papermill region has lost its young Sullivan, call at the Gallegan and look over the stock. He threatened among other things to shoot Downey.

August 24, 1885

Policeman Downey and Deputy Sheriff Carroll ran in J.W. Huyh yesterday. Huyh, evidently insane, was found on north Church St. fantastically attired in frontier costume and flourishing a variety of small arms.
December 18, 1885

Temporarily Bounced
Wm. S. Downey Suspended From the Police Force by Chief Blaney.

Tuesday evening Charles Holt a cigar maker and Wm. S. Downey, a policeman who was off duty, stepped into Frank McGraw's saloon. At the same time Emmanuel Luby entered in a half drunken condition and picking up a cigar box hit Holt on the side of the head. Holt asked for an explanation as they had no words and knew of no cause for the attack. Luby at once wanted to fight. Downey escorted him out of doors. Luby returned and said he could lick any policeman on the force and made a break for Downey who again threw him out on the walk. At this time Chief Blaney appeared and took Luby and sent him home. Yesterday morning the chief released Downey from duty and the case will be investigated at the meeting council next.
June 4,1886

Wearing a vest Louis Schilling leans nonchalantly against the facade of his market with (from right to left) grandson Guy (son of Gus), son Gus, son Walter, possibly grandson Arthur (son of the oldest Schilling brother, Charles), and possibly son Albert.

From the collection of the Kalamazoo Public Library

CHAPTER 1:
A Cruel Blow!
-Ends the Life of Louis Schilling
Kalamazoo Telegraph, March 21, 1893

GLANCING IN THE front window of the Schilling Market as he passed, Fred Zeeb expected to see his young acquaintance Bert Cave busy at work. What he found instead was the sole inhabitant and proprietor Louis Schilling engaged at his desk in the small office at the rear of the market. Although some distance and two windows separated them, the respected butcher was well known to Fred and easily identified. With his friend Bert apparently on an errand or at lunch, and thinking nothing of Mr. Schilling tending to business in his own shop, Fred carried on to dinner, unaware that he would be the last person, save one, to see Louis alive. Across the street in the barbershop of the gregarious Beau Hackley, the barber's assistant dozed peacefully with Beau having departed to a dinner engagement on Cooley St. Had he or any one of the business persons operating a store near the corner of Portage and Main Streets attentively observed the goings on of the day they would have seen a farmer enter the Schilling Market moments after Fred Zeeb passed. Later claiming to have arrived with the intent to sell Louis some beef, the farmer had first entered the Schilling Market alongside Ed Otto shortly after noon. Having found no one within to serve them, Ed Otto departed, presumably returning to his business as a shoe salesman. The farmer, still intent on negotiating the sale of his beef, departed only temporarily. With the noon hour nearly over he entered the market for the second time and was similarly unsuccessful in his attempt to find anyone within.

As he lingered in front of the market the farmer drew the attention of young William Ser Vaas who was an employee of Radiker's Plumbing one building north of the Schilling Market. As he was well acquainted with the Schilling family William volunteered to assist the farmer with his inquiry and proceeded into the market. Venturing through the vacant shop William opened the icebox before peeking into the back alley by way of the rear door. With both locations equally deficient of clues as to the whereabouts of any of the Schilling Market employees, William proceeded to the one room left unexplored. Opening the door to the small office in the rear of the market he scanned the dimly lit room. A moment later, the young man bolted from the market pale-faced and frantically looking for someone to whom he could report his grisly discovery.

A Great Day of Sport: Policeman Downey Bests Seven Competitors in a Boat Race.

The boat race was for a distance of one mile straight away with eight contestants. Wm. Downey, the policeman was a hustler on the send off and got the best start. He took the lead and kept it.
July 30, 1886

Two Policemen Suspended
Charges Preferred Against Officers Downey and Dustin

That they visited a gambling room said to be run by Eugene Scott in the Gale block on North Burdick. Policeman Downey is accused of visiting said room, watching the playing, and participating in a game of faro.
September 9, 1886

A large petition was received asking the council to reinstate as members of the police force Messrs Downey and Dustin, believing they had been sufficiently punished
October 5, 1886

Will Downey is the new turnkey at the jail.
October 29, 1886

10

Smith Better This Morning

The man Jack Smith who was injured so severely yesterday, presumably by Frank Kountz, continued in so critical a condition after being removed to the jail, that deputy Sheriff Downey sat up with him all night. He was much better this morning.
March 4, 1887

Turnkey Downey Thwarts an Attempt to Break Jail

One of the most audacious attempts at jail delivery that was ever made in this city was made yesterday. Frank Wilson who was sentenced to four years in the state prison at Jackson by Judge Mills last Friday, procured one of the steel knives with which the prisoners are allowed to eat their meals. He managed to cut several notches in it, making a saw. With this he had been at work for some days sawing off the bars from one of the windows. When discovered by Turnkey Downey yesterday, he had managed to sever one of the bars and was sawing into a second one, which he had nearly succeeded in cutting in two. March 22, 1887

Artist's rendering of the first building occupied by the Kalamazoo Gazette in 1835. *From the collection of the Kalamazoo Public Library*

CHAPTER 2:
The First

Hard names at first and threat'ning words,
That are but noisy breath,
May grow to stones and naked swords,
To murder, and to death.

Isaac Watts

THE YEAR 1837 would see the Michigan territory admitted to the union as the 26th state and William P. Giddings operating a store in Gull Prairie just northeast of the recently renamed Village of Kalamazoo (originally titled Bronson the name was soon changed owing to the eccentric and somewhat disagreeable nature of its namesake, Titus Bronson). One morning, from within his store, Mr. Giddings heard the familiar snarl of his brother's dog, which had noticed another local mongrel approaching. Too often of late the rival dogs had been at each other's throats and quickly separated before dominance could be asserted. Today, Mr. Giddings thought as he exited his store, was the day for the two dogs to reach a satisfactory hierarchical understanding. As the two hounds snarled and snapped at one another in the dirt, Mr. Giddings and a small crowd looked on with indifference. From a short distance James Ayres overheard the commotion and soon discovered his dog engaged in combat with another, while a man he harbored great animosity towards looked on. What mania overcomes a man in a moment such as this I cannot say, but James Ayres was lost to madness. With brickbat in hand he approached the spectating Mr. Giddings and unceremoniously applied the weapon to his temple with great force. Before he fell to the ground, another, who happened to be close to the affray, caught Mr. Giddings in his arms. There, bleeding in the embrace of a neighbor, Mr. Giddings was struck several more times by his assailant. With his wrath satiated Ayres retreated, and the battered Mr. Giddings was brought to his home where medical attention was received. The final eight hours of Mr. Giddings' life were lived in a painful fog, and mercifully his agony was soon ended.

Bestowed with the ignominious title of the county's first recorded murderer, James Ayres was incarcerated pending trial. When the date finally arrived, he was presented before none other than the great Kalamazooian and future Governor of the State of Michigan, Judge Erasmus Ransom. Friends of William Giddings and the prosecution fervently argued in favor of capital punishment, but in the end James Ayres was given a sentence of three years imprisonment and a $1000 fine. In the execution of his sentence Ayres was incarcerated in Kalamazoo County's ramshackle jail, which at that time sat very near the mound in what is now Bronson Park. His first year of confinement was by all reports uneventful, with Ayres being described as an affable and even remorseful prisoner. Regardless of his captor's opinion of him, it appears that Ayres' opinion of captivity soon soured, and at some unknown and unwatched moment he made his escape without much difficulty; he was never seen or heard of in these parts again.

To Kalamazoo's shame, neighboring Van Buren County would not experience its first recorded murder until September of 1853, when John Melvin Reynolds was convicted of murdering Clark Lewis. After a lengthy oration on the value of life, and excoriation of the convicted man, Judge Pratt handed down a sentence of life imprisonment. A much more fitting punishment for the senseless dowsing of another's life some might say.[2]

---

2 This chapter's epigraph accompanied the November 1837 Kalamazoo Gazette account of William Giddings' murder.

A Crazy Man Placed in Jail

Just after 11 O'clock today a Hollander who was on the walk at the corner of Rose and Main streets showing signs of insanity, and violence, was seized by Officer Downey as the man was about to attack him. A severe encounter ensued, in which Officer Downey and Special Policemen J.H. Harper were scratched somewhat. With the help of others the maniac was lodged in jail. April 26, 1887

Downey as a Star Lecturer

A colored lady brought to the jail this morning her incorrigible eight year old son who, it is greatly feared, will some day bring down her gray hairs in sorrow to the grave. He is disobedient, runs away from school and makes her a great deal of trouble. She left him at the jail and desired him to be locked up for a short period for reformatory purposes. Turnkey Downey gave the young man a scorching curtain lecture and released him with sundry warnings, which ought to have a stimulating effect on his moral nature. May 17, 1887

Downey Took Him In

Herbert Congdon lives in the fifth ward, near the handle factory, and last evening he went home and it is claimed drove his wife, mother in-law and father in-law out of the house. In response Officers Doan, Warren, Cairns, and Rice took a flying trip to the scene of war. They supposed that tramps had tackled the handle work's night watchman, but arriving found that at the Congdon domicile there had been trouble but all was quiet and they returned stating that "they had all gone to bed". The women followed their call for the police up town and scoured the city for a "cop," but could not find one. They then took possession of police headquarters, but soon went to the jail and the Downey Bros accompanied them home. Deputy Sheriff Downey attempted to get in the house, but Herbert Congdon held the fort and threatened dire vengeance on whomsoever entered. Downey, however, crawled into a window, took two flatirons from Congdon and took him to jail. The iron weapons of warfare are at the recorder's courtroom. It is a very cold day when Downey gets left.
December 24, 1887

Officer Downey was telephoned to from Constantine Saturday afternoon to arrest Wm. Plank alias Fred Roofe, charged with embezzlement. In less than twenty minutes the chap was jailed.
February 13, 1888

Deputy Sheriff Downey going along the street Sunday was attacked by a savage dog and the result was a torn pair of new $10 pants. This officer neglected his duty that he did not kill the beast at once.
February 14, 1888

Downtown Kalamazoo as it looked in 1883. The Schilling Market occupied the building just west of the P in Portage.
Library of Congress, Geography and Map Division

CHAPTER 3:
The Scene

"One of the most horrible cases of human butchery in the annals of crime"

Detroit Free Press, March 22, 1893

OPENING HER FRONT door onto Portage St. Mrs. Whitcomb prepared to see her daughter off to school following their noon meal. In doing so she was puzzled to see a short, thickset man in a snuff-brown suit of clothes, with a red face and bulging eyes, hurriedly pass by. As she watched, the man she would later describe as having an awful and ugly expression quickly made his way south with one hand in his pocket, turning multiple times to look back over his shoulder towards the Schilling Market. Thinking his behavior strange Mrs. Whitcomb mentioned the man to her husband, with both unaware that just seconds before William Ser Vaas had discovered the mutilated body of Louis Schilling. Like the rest of Kalamazoo the Whitcombs' obliviousness to the incident would be short-lived, as within minutes word of the grisly crime had begun to spread like hot smoke throughout the city.

Standing mere feet from a scene that was later described as horrible beyond description, 29-year-old Albert Schilling was presented with the unenviable experience of more closely inspecting his father's mutilated body. At the time that his father's corpse had been discovered Albert was assisting with the trading of some horses at Mr. William's barn. It was there that Albert was located by Burt Cave, who had returned to the Schilling Market moments after William Ser Vaas had made his discovery. After rushing to the market Albert found that his sister-in-law and her neighbors, the Engles, who all lived in apartments above the market, had preceded him in arriving. While all of those present had already taken a distant cursory glance into the office before he'd arrived, they lacked the will or constitution to investigate further, leaving Albert as the hapless volunteer.

As Albert hesitantly approached the dimly lit office his father's hat and recently lighted pipe could be seen lying haphazardly on the floor just inside of the doorway. As he stepped past these items and into the small 5 x 8 foot room, a single window, which opened into the market, provided just enough light so that Albert could make out the crumpled body of his now deceased father to his left. With the right shoulder against the south wall and the left against a small stove, the body lay face up in a manner as if it had slumped into the corner from a seated position; the high stool that accompanied the nearby small desk being his father's likely previous roost. Still-warm blood covered the body and the floor with small spurts visible where they had landed on the stove, the stool, and Louis's left hand. Moving to his father's side Albert found that in addition to what he could now see were multiple deep lacerations to the throat, his father's left ear had been mashed, with the lower half having been nearly completely severed from the head. Albert could also see that while his father's apron was in place, the vest pocket underneath appeared to have been pulled out. Lifting the blood-soaked apron Albert searched beneath and found that the pocketbook normally kept within was conspicuously missing. Before removing himself from the increasingly upsetting scene Albert found two other items of note: The first was that his father's pants pocket still contained $2.02. The second was a bruise on his father's left forearm, which Albert and his family would later theorize had been defensive in origin; although others would point out that striking the stove as he fell could also have accounted for both the bruising on Louis's arm and the damage to his ear.

Withdrawing from the office Albert found that a large crowd of curious onlookers had filled the walk and parts of Portage St. in front of the market. Patrolman Kremer, who had been at his post on the corner of Burdick and Main Streets when word of the incident had reached him, had been the first officer to arrive. As the patrolman attempted to control the host of spectators who intrusively peered and pressed against the market windows, August Schilling locked the front door. August, or "Gus", was the third oldest of Louis Schilling's eight children and lived above the Schilling Market with his wife and young son and daughter, a home Louis had often visited on his lunch hour in order to spend time with his grandchildren. Gus had spent his noon hour at home on this particular day and had descended the stairs that flanked the Schilling Market in order to return to his employ at Stern and Co. on East Main St. just ten minutes before the discovery of his father's body. Gus had not been back at work but a few minutes before he was located and beckoned home. He now found himself standing bewildered in the middle of an increasingly chaotic scene, aware that he may have been upstairs enjoying his dinner while his father lay dying below. As he and Albert discussed the distressing situation, a growing team of Kalamazoo professionals arrived at the Schilling Market to begin the daunting task of piecing together the puzzle of their father's death.

In their official capacities it was local physician William Bosman and Coroner Edwin Burdick who arrived to helm the medical investigation. Dr. Bosman made it his initial priority to confirm what the Schilling family already suspected; that Louis had been murdered rather than committing suicide. In hindsight this may seem an obvious deduction, but at the offset suicide may have actually been the more reasonable suspicion. The practice has grown increasingly rare, but in the 19th century it was not unusual for suicidal individuals to cut their own throats. This method of ending one's life was so common in fact that just six days before Louis Schilling's body was found an article entitled *Blundering Work* was published in the *Gazette*. Within, one unnamed physician detailed how he was forced to re-cut the throat of a patient in order to release pressure and insert a breathing tube. It seems the poor despondent man had attempted to end his life, missed the vein, and instead severed his windpipe resulting in a clogged trachea. Reflecting on this experience the physician posited this bit of advice: "If would be suicides would kindly sever their jugular vein instead of their windpipe they'd accomplish their purpose with greater certainty, and save themselves and physicians much trouble." Poor taste and cold indifference aside, the views expressed in this article highlight a significant point; in 1893 it would have been much more likely for a resident of Kalamazoo to cut their own throat than have it cut by someone else. Coroner Burdick could certainly attest to this fact as in his short time as coroner this was not the first time he'd investigated a body with a comparable wound, Mrs. Belle Talbot having committed such an act on herself the previous summer.

However, in contrast to the Talbot case there was a plethora of readily discoverable signs that indicated that Louis Schilling had not chosen the method of his demise. The most substantial of which was not discovered until after Dr. Bosman had completed his initial findings and coroner Burdick had formed a coroner's jury. Made of a group of well-respected men that included John McBride, J.W. Struthers, Herbert Tyson, Duke Waud, W.H. Stockdale, and George Locke, the coroner's jury viewed the crime scene and together with Coroner Burdick and Dr. Bosman made a decision as to the nature of the case. Considering that Louis Schilling's neck had been slashed more than once, with one of the wounds cutting so deeply as to damage the bone, the coroner's jury unanimously agreed that the case before them was that of a murder. Following their decision the body of Louis Schilling was prepared for movement to the coroner's office. It was during this process—as the body was lifted away from the wall—that three deep gashes were found in the back of Louis's head, two of which had penetrated his skull a full inch. Retrieving Louis's cap from the floor a large hole was found, which corresponded with one of the wounds on his head. These discoveries left those present with no doubt that some unknown fiend had struck him over the head before slashing his throat and absconding with his pocketbook.

Insurance Agent Gives Downey a Chase but "Will" Gets Him all the Same.

On Saturday last Deputy Sheriff Will Downey struck the trail of Foresman whose frauds among the guileless and unsuspecting has proved a moneymaking tour up to within brevity of time. That officer pursued him to White Pigeon and on Saturday evening the game was snared. Mr. Downey did not have a very full description of the man and had been in White Pigeon some time without seeing anything that looked like Foresman and he was about to take the train to another point, when lo! there passed him on the street a slick young man, with a plug hat, well dressed, head up and apparently intent on some business mission. It struck Officer Downey at once that this was his man, but as he was not sure he followed on in his wake till he arrived at the station. Here Foresman stepped to the baggage room to get his trunk. That was enough for Will; he had seen the trunk before. So he starts to go for his game. Foresman, who had evidently been posted, saw Downey and started to run, Downey after him. It was a hot chase. In going through a crowd of people at the station Foresman ran against a man and this checked his speed and before he could get by Downey had his clinchers on him. The fellow hollerd "murder" "help" "he's a sand bagger" "will you see me robbed!" still pulling Downey along trying to get into the hotel. It was a hard tussle and the tide of battle was first with the one and then the other. At his cries two men started to his assistance when Downey very emphatically told them he was an Officer and was arresting this man for crime. He then got his hands on Foresman and choked him into subjection. He then placed handcuffs on the captured individual. March 26, 1888

Officer Downey went out to the paper mill this forenoon to take into custody Thos. Fitzpatrick alleged to be insane, as many of his recent acts seem to prove. Last night he made a savage attack upon his wife and would have killed her but for the interference of others. Officer Downey secured Mr. F. and took him to jail.
March 20, 1888

The names presented for constables this year are exceptionally strong. William S. Downey, is recognized as one of the best criminal officers the county ever had. He has push and energy and has had abundant experience.
March 30, 1889

Officer Downey grabbed a 250 pound drunken man as he was reeling into a baby cab Friday. He caught him just in time.
June 30, 1889

Benjamin Franklin Orcutt - Sheriff of Kalamazoo 1854–58 & 1866–67.
From the collection of the Kalamazoo Public Library

CHAPTER 4:
Real Peril

"A Sheriff Mortally Shot"
Boston Journal, December 04, 1867

ESCRIBED AS BEING too small, poorly organized, and so insecure as to be surprising in its ability to hold anyone in, the state of the county jail in 1867 was widely seen as a local disgrace. Having served in two wars and on his second term as sheriff, Colonel Benjamin Franklin Orcutt was as capable as any man to undertake the unenviable position of maintaining the security of such a porous facility. Indeed, while serving as deputy sheriff in 1859, Benjamin Orcutt had intervened as cow thieves John Lushpaugh and David Bouker and burglar George Day made their escape through a hole in the jail roof. Firing his revolver as Lushpaugh and Day leapt to the ground, Deputy Sheriff Orcutt was able to catch Bouker before he could likewise leap to freedom. After he'd forced Bouker back into the hole from whence he had extricated himself, Deputy Sheriff Orcutt had set about returning the other two men to their cells.

In November 1867, Sheriff Orcutt found himself housing a trio of disreputable characters by the names of Dutch Fritz, Black Bill, and Bob Taylor; the prisoners having been arrested after brazenly breaking into the Kalamazoo treasurer's office and blowing open the safe therein. Not finding their newfound accommodation to their liking the three criminals quickly set about implementing the manufacture of their escape. To his credit the ever-vigilant sheriff made it his business to prevent their departure and within his first week of housing the criminals found them attempting to covertly burn holes in the outer hall doors in an effort to loosen the bolts that secured them. Paradoxically, had Sheriff Orcutt not been so attentive, and the trio made their escape during this initial attempt, it is unlikely that the life of the esteemed sheriff would have come to a tragic end just three weeks later.

On the night of December 3rd 1867, Sheriff Orcutt was awoken by an irregular noise while asleep in his home adjacent to the jail. Seizing his revolver and hastening towards the source of the disturbance, he arrived to find two men endeavoring to pass a set of tools to their incarcerated confederates. In a commanding voice the sheriff shouted for the pair to stop. His commands were ignored, and, having recognized known criminal Hugh Darragh as one of the men, Sheriff Orcutt fired his revolver. Small amounts of blood later found along the escape route indicate that at least one of the sheriff's shots had found its mark, although the damage was apparently little more than superficial and did little to slow the fleeing men. With resolve and determination Sheriff Orcutt engaged in a spirited chase that quickly saw him shortening the distance between himself and the fleeing men. As Hugh Darragh ran on as quickly as he could from the encroaching sheriff, his partner began to suffer the effects of asthma and darted behind a large burr oak near the alley in the rear of Bartlett's bookstore. Unaware that one of the men lingered nearby Sheriff Orcutt rushed fearlessly onward. As the unsuspecting sheriff approached, the hidden asthmatic produced a previously concealed pistol and, leaning out from his position behind the tree, fired three times.

It was reported that Sheriff Orcutt, having been struck

once just above the lung, shouted, "Murder!" and staggered back towards his home. Mrs. Orcutt, nearly overcome with grief, met the wounded sheriff and, along with David Fisher and George Taylor, helped him into the Orcutt home. News of the attempted jailbreak and the subsequent shooting quickly spread throughout the village. As attempts were made to unravel the confusing situation a search of the jail cells turned up a revolver that had apparently been successfully passed to the prisoners by the men who had gotten away. With word spreading and fury growing, a large crowd formed in the yard outside the jail. Many present called for the quick and violent end of the prisoners still lodged within who were seen as the instigators of the affair. Others argued against such archaic forms of mob justice, and soon calmer heads prevailed. With the crowd having tentatively reached an agreement not to engage in rash action an impromptu meeting was led by General Dwight May, with whom Sheriff Orcutt had served in the war. Although questions remained regarding what exactly had transpired, it was unanimously agreed that all effort should be made to find and arrest the two men who had caused such grievous injury to the dying sheriff.

With one of the wanted men having already been identified by Sheriff Orcutt as Hugh Darragh, it was soon determined that the other man accompanying him was hardened criminal Stephen Boyle. To the good of Kalamazoo's reputation neither man was a native of Michigan, they were in fact exports of that great metropolis to the east, New York City. Boyle had begun his criminal career as a butcher-cart thief and a leader of the Nineteenth Street Gang. When his many unlawful activities made things in the east too "warm" for him, Boyle and his gang had moved their operations to Chicago. Predictably, Boyle soon found himself housed in Illinois' Joliet Prison. With their leader incarcerated the rest of the gang headed to southwest

Michigan. Eager to follow, Boyle soon escaped from prison and united with fellow criminal Hugh Darragh shortly thereafter. The two men arrived in Kalamazoo in the fall of 1867 to find their three friends locked up in the county jail. Having botched their attempted jail-break, and now wanted for murder, the two men returned to more familiar locales in the east.

After returning to NYC it took just one month for Hugh Darragh, who was going by the name William Hyatt at the time, to slip up, and he was apprehended while attempting to pick pockets in Manhattan. One very adept and vigorous detective from Chicago named Dickson had joined the search for the killers and had tracked the men to New York. With Darragh in custody Detective Dickson was able to positively identify him as one of the men responsible for Sheriff Orcutt's death. Michigan Governor Henry H. Crapo then wired New York City requesting extradition. Complying, officers brought Darragh to the train station, and under the watchful eye of Detective Dickson he was soon Michigan bound. En-route Darragh expressed fears of being lynched, but rather than an angry mob the only adversary he faced upon arriving in Kalamazoo was a judge. Hugh Durragh was convicted as an accomplice in the murder of Sheriff Orcutt and was given six years in Jackson State Prison where he subsequently died.

Although many celebrated the apprehension of Darragh there was a temporary unintended negative consequence. The significant newspaper coverage of his arrest had caused Stephen Boyle to grow increasingly afraid of his impending imprisonment. With lawmen closing in Boyle went into hiding and was able to avoid what had seemed like his imminent capture. Fortunately for those who pursued him, Boyle's criminal nature soon got the better of him. It would not be long before his propensity for crime would again bring Stephen Boyle within view of law enforcement.

Stephen Boyle, aka Gus Shaw, aka Edward Francis, aka Edward Barrett, aka Richard Peyton, tempted fate at every turn and was soon the main suspect in three of the heaviest highway robberies undertaken in 1868. It wasn't until he shot and nearly killed an officer during an attempted jewelry store robbery in February of 1869 that he was finally re-apprehended. In an effort to avoid extradition to Michigan Boyle proved willing to confess to nearly any crime with which he had been associated in New York, including the assault with brass knuckles on a Mr. Waterhouse in the Bowery the summer prior. Although Kalamazoo Sheriff Wells immediately proceeded east by train to secure the captured murderer, New York chose to enact its privilege and argued that Michigan would save money if Boyle was tried in New York where he was facing two twenty-year sentences. Although many in Michigan opposed the decision, Boyle remained in New York where he was sent to Sing Sing Prison for twenty-five years.

As disappointed as the people of Kalamazoo were by the decision not to bring Boyle to Michigan they were doubly aggrieved when, on May 14, 1875, he escaped from prison for the second time in his life. If Boyle was considered a well-known local criminal prior to this escape, he was infamous thereafter. In an elaborate plan that would be talked about well into the twentieth century Stephen Boyle and four other men were able to seize a train engine within the Sing Sing Prison enclosure and throttle it to freedom. The implementation of the plan began with the creation of wooden pistols complete with black paint and silver accents. Their "weapons" concealed under their clothing, the inmates waited until an opportune moment allowed them to rush the train that passed through the prison yard. Brandishing the wooden replicas they threatened the train's fireman and engineer who, believing the pistols to be the genuine article, willingly leapt from engine. While one of the convicts pulled the pin that connected the engine to the other cars, Boyle took the throttle in hand. With shots flying wildly in the direction of the departing locomotive, Boyle stoked the engine up to sixty miles an hour. While it took only minutes for the convicts to put significant distance between themselves and their pursuers, they had in fact blown out the cylinder head of the engine in their eagerness to escape. Slowly the engine de-accelerated and the men were eventually forced to abandon some ten miles from the prison. With the five convicts now on foot, Boyle partnered with fellow escapee Charles Fowler, and together the two men made their way to Missouri.

Artist's rendering of Stephen Boyle's "Thrilling escape from Sing Sing".
Professional Thieves and the Detective by Allan Pinkerton 1883

In August of 1875, three months after the now famous prison break, G.W. Walling, the superintendent of the New York City Police Department, received a letter. Within were the pictures of two men and a letter from St. Louis Chief of Police L. Hannigan, which read in part:

"Dear Sir,

Enclosed please find photographs of two men whom I arrested here on Saturday, with 'safe tools' in their possession. They are evidently professionals, and if you or any of your men know them I will be under obligations to you if you will furnish me with any information you may obtain regarding them."

Recognizing the two men straightaway as Boyle and Fowler, Superintendent Walling sent a return telegram wherein he made it clear that the men in question should be immediately transported back to New York so that they could be returned to their penal residence on the noble Hudson.

Once again residing within the walls of Sing Sing Stephen Boyle was nothing if not obstinate in the face of incarceration. Unable to find a way to exit the prison system under his own power, he soon devised a scheme to leave on a technicality. At some point in the early 1880s Boyle made the acquaintance of the convict in charge of the prison drug shop. Influencing the druggist through charm or threat he convinced the man to provide him with medication that would make him deathly ill, which he then began to regularly ingest. Owing to this dangerous ruse Boyle soon found himself in the prison hospital, and at his request a number of friends on the outside began to press for his sentence to be commuted; the argument being that he was dying and should be allowed to do so a free man. Remarkably, the man who was wanted for the murder of Sheriff Orcutt, had shot at least one other officer, was a suspect in numerous other crimes, and had twice escaped from prison was released in March of 1886. Free and no longer ingesting poison, Boyle's miraculous recovery was predictable, and he soon returned to his old ways.

After only two months of freedom he was arrested in New York City while attempting to pick pockets on a streetcar. For this crime Boyle was given a sentence of 3 ½ years, and in late 1886 he was transferred to the Clinton State Prison in Auburn, NY (the engineer of the train he was transported on just happened to be the same engineer that Boyle and his cohorts had held up and forced to jump during their escape some ten years before). While his sentence was short when compared to some that he had previously received, the Clinton State Prison officials were determined to see that Boyle found this the most disagreeable of all his stints in prison. Nearly permanently shackled hand and foot to the floor of his cell, the now aging criminal was given no opportunity to escape or even plot the manufacture of his discharge. This practice continued for nearly a full year, and somewhat unsurprisingly Stephen Boyle died in the late 1880s having been convicted of numerous crimes but never for the murder of Sheriff Benjamin Franklin Orcutt.

A team of horses attached to a wagon loaded with buckwheat and owned by C.G. Kleinstuck, who lives near the asylum, became frightened yesterday forenoon on east Main street and ran pell mell through Main Street adroitly dodging several vehicles in their flight. As they neared Rose street they were headed for a carriage near the Israel corner but William Dennison at the risk of his life rushed out and caught one of the horses by the head. They were getting the best of him when Hon. William S. Downey caught the other horse and the team were stopped.
December 20, 1889

Jumped In The River

If William S. Downey was ever rattled in his life he was last night. He started out with his fine gray horse in search of traces for the thief who stole Duke Wand's horse. He drove along the riverbank just south of the new iron bridge when the horse became frightened at a woman leading a cow and jumped to one side. Mr. Downey did not care to take a bath and jumped off the bank and turned the wagon bottom side up. The horse fell down and was just able to hold his head above water. Downey was more unnerved than he would be to meet a half dozen horse thieves. He ran and secured a boat without oars and was soon fast in the weeds and could not reach the horse. He telephoned to police headquarters for help and the patrol wagon, and tour officers responded but two boys waded out and cut the horse loose and drew out the wagon. The wagon was but little damaged. The police all "took something" on the hustling but rattled officer.
June 13, 1890

A Field Day Of Crime – A Large Grist of Criminals Landed in Jail

Early Tuesday morning Charles Ehrman notified Officer Downey that thieves had been through his chicken coop and taken several valuable fowls. The officer was soon on the track and found six chickens in a boiling pot. Samuel Cowell and Charles Hatch were both locked up in jail and will have a hearing before Judge Peck today.

A man who gave his name as Richard Hyland was gathered in by the police yesterday and his boodle, amounting to $70 in currency, $50 in gold and three silver dollars, a total of $123, was saved for him from the sharks who hang around the city. Officers Downey and Harper made the arrest.

July 04, 1890

William S. Downey

As the readers of the Gazette are well aware, William S. Downey is the democratic candidate for sheriff. He is also the candidate of the Patrons of Industry for the same office and there can be little question of his election. He is well known to the people of Kalamazoo County, both as a citizen and a criminal officer. When he starts out for a criminal he generally gets his man and there is no instance where one got away after he laid his hands on him. Among his most noted captures were the two safe blowers that attempted to blow the safe at the Spring and Axle works. The two safe blowers are now serving terms in states prison and Downey is the only officer that has captured that class of criminals in Kalamazoo County. He is strong with the workingmen and is the people's candidate and no amount of money used against him will turn that vote away. It will stand by him as the Old Guard did Napoleon. Wm. S. Downey was brought up on a farm and unlike his opponent is not a chronic office holder. When John Dix was holding soft government positions Downey was working by the month on a farm.

October 19, 1890

The boys are all going to vote for William Downey, because they say he is a hustler and never allows a guilty man to escape.

November 01, 1890

It's **Sheriff Downey!**
– He takes the office from Sheriff Dix
January 09, 1891

William S. Downey – Candidate for Sheriff
Kalamazoo Gazette, October 30, 1890

CHAPTER 5:
Sheriff Downey

"A Terror To Thieves and Crooks"
Kalamazoo Gazette, October 29, 1892

L IKE MANY EARLY inhabitants of this great county, William S. Downey Jr. began his life far afield. Born in Belfast, Ireland on March the 2nd 1852, an adolescent William found himself and younger brother and sister in the tow of their widower father as they immigrated west. Pausing briefly in Canada the family eventually moved to Michigan where in 1862 William Sr. acquired a small farm west of the village of Kalamazoo near Texas Corners. As a youth William Jr.'s build and character grew congruent to laborious life on a mid-western farm; likewise, his ambition grew proportionately with the burgeoning village of Kalamazoo. After acquiring an education in the local public school William enrolled at Kalamazoo College where he spent two years pursuing higher education; those efforts were cut short in 1872 when William Sr. died unexpectedly, forcing William to pursue financial rather than academic ends. After a short period working the family farm William found employment at the Michigan Asylum for the Insane where he spent the next four years working security and as a porter. This was followed by a two-year period of travel during which William explored the western United States. With his youthful appetite for travel and adventure satiated

William returned home to begin a career as a police officer that would numerously see him described as one of the best lawmen Kalamazoo had ever seen.

Smith The Velveteen Thief Arrested

Smith is one the celebrated velveteen thieves that escaped from Sheriff Dix. Sheriff Downey left for Virginia last evening. He has a photograph of the man, and if the man proves to be the right party, he will be brought to Kalamazoo and put in the cage, and it is safe to say that he will not again break out of the Kalamazoo jail.

June 07, 1891

Wool Thieves Caught

Sometime between Tuesday evening and Wednesday morning a thief or thieves entered Mr. Hugh Fraser's barn in the township of Oshtemo. Mr. Fraser at once notified Sheriff Downey and he was at work searching for the thieves. The Sheriff and Deputy Sheriff Charles Rickard traced them to Plainwell, where they secured their arrest.

June 26, 1891

Downey The Runner

Sheriff Downey and deputies have been busy at work on the burglarizing of the depot at Schoolcraft and traced them to Grand Rapids where the Sheriff had one McClellan apprehended by the city police force yesterday. Sheriff Downey went after his man yesterday afternoon and when they reached the G.R. & I. depot here the sheriff reached forward and McClellan made a break for the car door and jumped off the car on the east side and at the same time jerked the handcuff loose from his lame hand and started east. The sheriff gave chase east on Main Street and fired into the ground and commanded the escaped bird to stop, but he did not stop. He ran north on the Lake Shore track and east on Kalamazoo Avenue and fell as he entered a garden just east of the Second Baptist church, and here the officer gained on him and told him to stop. He stopped and was taken to jail. Sheriff Downey says that it will be the last time any man gets any the start of him.

July 01, 1891

Disturbers of the Peace Landed in Jail From the Lake

Everything had been quiet and orderly at Long Lake yesterday until between three and four O'clock. The chief trouble was bottled up and concealed in a "grip" down by the lake, where a little something could be obtained on the quiet. The sheriff raided the illegal land "bum boat" and emptied the contents into the lake after arresting James Clark for fighting. Others took a hand in disturbing the peace and the sheriff and Officers Bennett, Sweet, and Skinner landed a sextet of the offenders in the jail. Besides those mentioned above were John VanderPolder, Henry Sootsman, Geo. Babcock and T. Colligan.

August 21, 1891

During his tenure William Downey's administration earned praise from both sides of the political aisle and was largely seen as one of the most proficient in Kalamazoo's history. Unlike his predecessor, Sheriff Downey was able to prevent any prisoners from escaping the county jail; an accomplishment that as you read through this text you will realize is no small feat. In fact, he was instrumental in the returning to jail of a number of the prisoners who had made their escape in 1890 while under the supervision of Sheriff Dix. Sheriff Downey was also credited with the capture of a number of "professional" criminals, the likes of which had not been apprehended in Kalamazoo before. In 1907, William Downey would reminisce on his time as sheriff and recount the case of Sam Ashman as one of the most notable of his career. As demonstrated by the headlines of the day, William was not the only one to think so.

"One of the Best Captures of Crooks
Ever Made in this Part of the Country"
Kalamazoo Gazette, February 21, 1892

John Smith was first brought to the recorder's office in January of 1892 for stealing a coat. During the trial that followed Smith acted as his own defense attorney and confidently quizzed the witnesses brought against him. His apparent comfort as a defendant probably should have been an indication to those present of the man's true vocation. But owing to his loquacious ways, and a trick he had utilized during his crimes wherein he would switch hats or put a hat over his cap, Smith was not positively identified, and three members of the jury were unconvinced of his guilt. In mid-February 1892, Smith was released in the company of another crook named Charles

Hayes, and within days the two men would attempt some of the boldest burglarious raids the city had ever seen.

On the evening of February 20, 1892, the men began their criminal spree at the G, R, & I ticket office. As dusk settled Smith and Hayes smashed a window and unsuccessfully attempted to pry open the money drawer therein. They then moved on a short distance to the Cobb home on South Street but were frightened away as they contemplated how best to enter. The pair then approached the home of Walter Taylor in Eldridge Terrace where they were likewise frightened away. By this point in the evening the sheriff's office had received a number of calls from concerned citizens who all described two suspicious looking men lurking in the vicinity. After rushing to the area Sheriff Downey found that local businessman Herbert Tyson had detained one half of the suspicious duo. Charles Hayes was placed in cuffs and led to jail.

With his partner incarcerated John Smith had no intention of slowing his marathon of crime. Around midnight a call was received at the jail reporting that someone had entered McCullough's meat market on west North Street. Sheriff Downey quickly had his grey horse fitted and brought around. As he traveled down Main St. towards the disturbance the sheriff paused long enough to pick up Officer Merrill, who was considered a reliable man in difficult situations. The two men then set off towards the disturbance at so fast a clip that Officer Merrill feared they might wreck. As the two lawmen neared North St. they found an animated crowd gathered on the walk. Pausing, Sheriff Downey learned that after breaking into McCullough's meat market Smith had entered Balch's Grocery Store next door. When Mr. Balch had heard the sound of the intruder from the rooms above the store where he lived, he had risen to confront the culprit. When discovered by Mr. Balch, Smith had brandished a cleaver he had stolen from the meat market and threatened to "brain" the shopkeeper if he attempted to detain him. Backing off slightly Mr. Balch waited until Smith turned, and as soon as he did a piece of wood was fired at the thief's head. Smith then fled, and witnesses had seen him set off in the direction of the plank road. Upon hearing the criminal's path Sheriff Downey and Officer Merrill once again set off. As they approached William Glover's residence on Douglas Ave the two officers saw a dark figure dart from the walk into the shadows some distance in front of them. Stoking his horse fiercely onward Sheriff Downey's charger made a quarter mile in thirty seconds, and the two lawmen were soon at the spot where they had seen the mysterious character. Before the carriage could stop Officer Merrill leapt out and rushed towards the spot between the walk and the fence where he could now see a man lying flat. Still holding the reins of his horse with one hand Sheriff Downey followed, and together they attempted to apprehend Smith. As the criminal fought like a cornered animal, Officer Merrill was cut on the wrist. In response Sheriff Downey quickly landed a right-hander behind Smith's ear that sent him to the ground. The subdued criminal was then loaded into the rig and escorted back to the jail. Although he attempted to toss off his hat and replace it with another while on the way, no trick of Smiths would see him escape prosecution on this occasion. He was promptly sentenced to ten years in Jackson Prison, and it was learned shortly thereafter that his real name was Sam Ashman, a well-known Detroit criminal who had previously escaped from Ionia State Prison.

Sheriff Downey Put in a Busy Day Yesterday

A crowd of Battle Creek toughs were on a tear at Vicksburg Sunday and assaulted Broncho John who was there with his wild west company. They hit Broncho John and he demolished a lantern over the head of one of the crowd and drove them all out of the depot. Warrants were issued for the assailants by Justice French yesterday, and Sheriff Downey arrested four of them at Battle Creek at once.

September 15, 1891

Another Good Catch

Sheriff Downey returned Saturday eve from Detroit with Albert Zallves who stole the two fine watches from the Commercial house last Tuesday. This thief is a New York crook. He came here last Monday and registered as "Albert Zaller." Both watches have been recovered and this thief is on his way to Jackson prison.

April 22, 1892

An Old Crook

Solomon Richardson's grocery store at Vicksburg was burglarized Wednesday night. The description of the man who was supposed to have committed the crime tallied with that of Frank Casey an old-time crook, and Sheriff Downey after a long search found him just outside the city and locked him in jail. Some four years ago Sheriff Downey arrested Casey for burglarizing mint lines store in this city and he was sent to Ionia house of correction. The next job he was in and was caught was burglarizing Snyder store at Schoolcraft. Sheriff Downey caught him and he went to Jackson for two years.

May 13, 1892

Nabbed For Swindling

The Gazette recently contained an account of the alleged swindling operations of George Anderson an alleged attorney at law who secured $30 from Martin Justice, an old veteran. Sheriff Downey proceeded to trace him up, and he followed him to several towns with a warrant charging him with obtaining money by false pretenses and representing himself as a lawyer. He was arrested at Athens, Michigan and is now in jail here. He is a shrewd chap and his arrest is only another evidence that few crooks get away from Sheriff Downey.
July 29, 1892

Gathering Them In

Sheriff Downey is always at work on some case of crookedness and has recovered another set of harness stolen from Mr. Hazard of Wakeshma. He has now recovered all that was stolen from his barn on May 28 last except a blanket. The sheriff is of the opinion that there is an organized gang of thieves who have been working in southern Michigan and he is gradually gathering them in.
September 14, 1892

When William Downey took office in 1891, the presence in Kalamazoo of a competent sheriff's department could not have come at a better time as the occurrence of "serious" crimes had steadily risen in recent years. When Barnum & Baileys made their way to Kalamazoo in August of 1892, the chief of detectives employed by the show remarked that he had never seen so many crooks. There were also concerns that Chicago was loading criminals onto trains bound for Kalamazoo in an effort to clean up the city before the 1893 World's Fair. Still, even in the face of criminal activity that had increased in both frequency and severity, confidence in the Kalamazoo sheriff remained high. Given these facts it is unsurprising that, upon discovering that Louis Schilling had been murdered, the community would turn to William Downey.

When notified of the murder, William quickly sent word to Doctor Herman Ostrander of the asylum requesting that he meet him at the scene. William then hastened to the Schilling Market where he found that Officers Merrill and Sweet had already begun a cursory search of the premises. Significantly, the two officers had determined that none of the numerous blades on hand in the market appeared to have been used in the crime, and none were found to be missing. These facts were verified by twenty-year-old Walter Schilling, who worked with his father and had returned to the market from his dinner at the Schilling family home to find the initial stages of the investigation underway. William was also informed that after his initial efforts to control the crowd, Patrolman Kremer had discovered that the money drawer in the front of the market had not been molested and still contained the expected amount of currency within. With a sketch forming in his mind of what had transpired, William departed the market through the rear door. Scouring the alleyways, the outhouses, and the neighboring buildings William soon found a set of tracks left by a man wearing about a no. eight or nine-sized shoe. As he followed the tracks William discovered that they passed by the rear of Mr. Hubbard's rookery next to the market and ended in the alley where the mysterious individual appeared to have climbed over a shed of about five feet in height. The point where this individual had then jumped down from the shed on the other side and crossed behind a small building before entering the yard were clearly visible. After William alerted the others to his discovery Officer Merrill joined in the search and soon found return footprints in the alley where a man had been on the run in the opposite direction of the tracks that William had discovered.

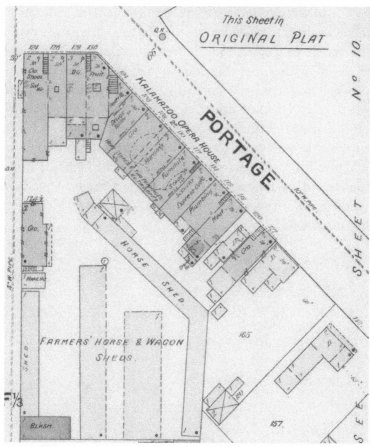

1891 fire insurance map showing the maze of alleys, sheds, and outbuildings behind the Schilling Market at 118 Portage St.
Library of Congress, Geography and Map Division

With officers quite literally trailing the footprints of the suspected murderer the investigation seemed to be off to a promising start. Unfortunately, and to the chagrin of many, William Downey was no longer the sheriff of Kalamazoo. He had lost his bid for re-election in November of 1892 and relinquished the office to William Vosburg in January of

1893. Sheriff Vosburg was not in Kalamazoo at the time of the murder, but upon his return later that afternoon William Downey's role in the investigation was ended.

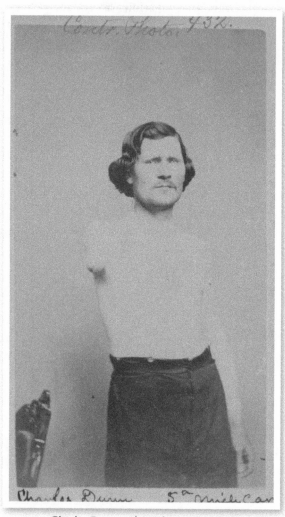

Charles Dunn, 5th Michigan Cavalry.
Liljenquist Family Collection (Library of Congress).

CHAPTER 6:
Three Cheers for Dunn
National Republican, May 27, 1864

S IX MILES NORTH of the Confederate capital of Richmond, near an inn called Yellow Tavern, the 5th Michigan Cavalry clashed with a tired and outnumbered Rebel force. Late in the afternoon, after hours of fighting in the pouring rain, men of the 5th were surprised to see a Confederate officer ride to an exposed spot within rifle range. One opportunistic Union Soldier not keen to lose such a prospect quickly fired but missed. Remarking coolly that the shot had been, "Too high, and too far to the left," Charles Dunn had the air of a man who thought himself capable.

"Say, old Dunn, what do you know about shooting?" remarked a fellow Soldier.

Stepping forward a few feet Dunn explained that he had served two years in the Berdan sharpshooters before joining the 5th. Their skepticism quickly giving way to optimism his fellow Soldiers watched as Dunn rested his long-range rifle upon a fence and fired. In the distance, through the rain and chaos of battle, Dunn's target threw up both hands, stretched out his arms, and fell from his horse. Turning nonchalantly to his commander, Dunn exclaimed, "Colonel, there's a spread eagle for you."

Although the identity of the fallen rebel officer was unknown at that time, Dunn became an instant favorite with the men, and his name spread throughout Custer's brigade. With the tide of the battle now firmly in their favor the Union forces pushed forward until they controlled the very ground where Dunn's target had been struck. A short distance away, on the summit of a hill, sat a small house. As Union Soldiers approached they discovered a trail of blood leading through the front door where a wounded man had apparently been carried. Turning to the old woman who lived within one Michigander questioned, "Whose blood is that, Aunty?"

To which she replied, "That is General Jeb Stuart's blood."

Hesitant to accept her account of the origin of the gore, Union Soldiers thoroughly interrogated the old woman regarding her shocking revelation. Unwavering in her assertions the woman replied that she knew Jeb Stuart by sight and it was most certainly the general who had been the source of the blood; a ball having entered his right side and exited out his left. Apprehension lingered with the men as rumors of General Jeb Stuart's demise had previously spread, with the Confederate cavalry hero always reemerging very much alive. It was not until the Richmond papers reached brigade command a few days later that the 5th Michigan Cavalry received confirmation that General Jeb Stuart was *Dunn* for. At least that's how the papers told it...

Charles Dunn returned to Kalamazoo after the war having gained a legend and lost an arm. Although rumors continued to swirl regarding the now disabled Soldier who had shot a Confederate officer, credit for shooting General Jeb Stuart had eventually been attributed to another. Regardless of the facts surrounding Jeb Stuart's death it is an undisputable fact that news reports crediting Dunn with the shooting had been circulated from Washington D.C. to the prairies of Kansas. There is also no doubt that people in the south read those accounts, and there were at least some who considered Dunn a great enemy of the Confederacy.

On the night of May 16, 1869, a number of men were drinking and carrying on in the saloon of Pat Reynolds on North Burdick Street. Among them were the one-armed Dunn and a tall, redheaded stranger whom no one present had seen before. Having arrived in Kalamazoo within the day the man appeared to have nearly immediately befriended Dunn. As the two whiled away the hours together, the stranger, who drank very little himself, plied Dunn with drinks while also stroking his ego. The visibly pleased Dunn continued to drink and tell stories with his new companion until night gave way to early morning and saloonkeeper Reynolds attempted to empty his establishment. As the men reluctantly finished their drinks one of Dunn's actual friends made a comment that Dunn was putting on a good many airs, as he and his new friend had kept their own company the majority of the evening. Feigning offence at the friendly ribbing the tall stranger flourished a revolver and exclaimed that he was a friend of Dunn's and proposed to stand by him. As the men jostled towards the street a sensible and by all accounts well-respected man named James McKinney approached the stranger and instructed him to put away his weapon or he would be forced to involve the law. In a turn equally shocking and unanticipated the tall stranger quickly turned to Charles Dunn and discharged his firearm before turning to James McKinney and likewise shooting him. The tall stranger then quickly ran off without anyone present knowing even his first name. As unexpected and inexplicable as the shooting first appeared there were those in Kalamazoo who felt that the truth was evident; a southern assassin had traveled to Kalamazoo to even the score on behalf of the Confederacy.

With Charles Dunn dead and James McKinney soon to follow Sheriff Wells was left with the very difficult task of tracking the unnamed double murderer. With no clues other than the eyewitness testimony of inebriated men it appeared that the tall stranger had made his escape back to the safety of the south; that was until the 21st of July when another double shooting occurred in Beloit, WI. It seems that officers in Beloit had been made aware of an attempted burglary on the evening of the 20th and in the course of their duties had located a tall stranger sometime around 1:00 the following morning. While leading the sinister-looking man to jail on suspicion, he had broken free, pulled a revolver, and shot Officers Hawley and Johnson. Although the perpetrator had initially escaped, it was only three days later, on the 24th, that a man named James Cotter, who matched the shooter's description, was arrested in Milwaukee, WI. When arrested, it was noted that the tall, dark Cotter not only fit the description of the Beloit shooter but also fit the description of the man wanted in connection with the double murder in Kalamazoo. Cotter was quickly transported to Beloit and word was sent to Sheriff Wells who immediately boarded a train for Wisconsin.

Rather unwisely Sheriff Wells did not bring any of the witnesses to the Dunn and McKinney murders with him to Wisconsin, and the initial identification of Cotter as the murderer was confused. It eventually transpired that Sheriff Wells was able to determine that James Cotter was not the man he was after. In point of fact, James Cotter was also not the man Beloit was after. And as far as anyone knows James Cotter was not an assassin, murderer, or criminal of any kind. He was in fact a sailor with a somewhat passing resemblance to two separate wanted men. The man whom the people of Beloit desperately sought for the wounding of two officers was Frank Leonard, alias Johnson, alias McMullan, alias Flanders, alias Gale, and alias several other names. Leonard was a longtime criminal who had done time in Detroit and later a prison in Wisconsin where he was given an early release in exchange for enlisting in the Union Army. En route to begin his service Leonard had "jumped" and made his way to Tennessee, where he promptly robbed a bank of $10,000 in gold. He was then arrested, and after again inexplicably securing his release he traveled to Iowa where he was arrested for burglary and for shooting a doctor. Having served only three years for his exploits in Iowa Leonard made his way to Wisconsin where he would eventually have the aforementioned encounter with officers in Beloit. In December of '69, Frank Leonard was captured in Chicago by detective Robert Kenny of the firm of Tutle & Co. He was then returned to Beloit to stand trial. While Beloit was able to locate and prosecute the man who had shot two men on their streets, Kalamazoo never was. The anonymous "Confederate assassin" who had so brazenly committed a double murder in Kalamazoo would remain unidentified.

Looking north towards Main from Portage Street c1892. Gus
Schilling's employer, Stern & Co., occupied the building with the white
awning in the center of the photo.
From the collection of the Kalamazoo Valley Museum

CHAPTER 7:
The First Pointer

"There is only one clue as to the murderer"
Jackson Citizen, March 22, 1893

J UST AS MRS. Whitcomb had not immediately understood the potential implication of the strange man she had seen pass her home minutes after the murder, so too had section hand Patrick Flynn not immediately realized the significance of the conversation he'd had less than one hour later. Working on the Michigan Central tracks west of the city near the asylum, Patrick Flynn noticed William "Bill" White approaching shortly before 2 p.m. As the conspicuous dark-skinned string butcher approached, Flynn could see that Bill had blood on his hands, clothing, and boots. Before he passed Bill turned to Flynn and rather nonchalantly remarked, "Well, goodbye. I'm going away and never coming back." When Flynn inquired about his destination, Bill's response varies depending on the source and was either that he was going to Chicago, that there was probably a warrant out for his arrest, and if caught he would be killed, or that he was going to Chicago and he had to hurry as he supposed there was now a warrant out for him. The two then said their good days, and Bill carried on out of town with Flynn thinking little of the exchange.

As word of the Schilling murder had not reached him at the time that he encountered Bill White, Patrick Flynn may be forgiven for not thinking more of the aforementioned conversation. As previously mentioned, Bill White was a string butcher, and the presence of blood on his clothing would not have been unexpected. Bill White's reputation as an individual on the wrong side of the law also preceded him. During his time as a string butcher Bill White had worked in most of the slaughterhouses in the Kalamazoo area and had consequently been arrested for stealing from nearly all of them. Bill was also quick to flourish a knife or weapon, with his first serious offence occurring in '87 when he'd threatened to "carve" a traveling man who dared intervene as Bill was holding up a small boy for pocket change. After the incident was reported officers found Bill in a saloon and attempted to arrest him. He then reportedly pulled a knife and threatened to do to the officers what he had threatened to do to the traveling man. After a short standoff Bill was subdued, and two large knives were removed from his person. Albert Schilling would report after the murder of his father that he'd previously had a similar altercation with Bill White when the latter pulled a knife and threatened to kill him. Albert stated that he'd then struck Bill White over the head with a gambrel, and Mr. Terrill had tossed Bill out of the slaughterhouse in which they were working. Bill White's most serious conviction took place in '91 when he and John Hopkins gravely assaulted Ed Walker, who it was said nearly lost his lip after the pair struck him in the face with a board. This crime resulted in a yearlong prison sentence for both Bill and John Hopkins. Upon being convicted John expressed his desire to separate himself from the "fighting" members of the community and vowed that upon his release he would find himself a small farm in the country where he could avoid trouble as much as possible. It does not appear that Bill White ever made such a resolution, and after his release Bill was arrested no less than three times in 1892. His most recent conviction prior to the Schilling murder was a charge of drunkenness in February 1893, which saw him spend the majority of the month in jail.

When Patrick Flynn later heard about the attack at the Schilling Market, he realized just how suspicious the interaction he'd had with Bill White was and reported it to authorities. Shortly thereafter it was revealed that Patrolman Todd had also seen Bill moving west on the tracks shortly after the murder. Given the aforementioned incidence of criminality in Bill's past, and the seemingly unbelievable coincidence that no less than two people had seen him fleeing the city shortly after Louis Schilling was found murdered, Bill White quickly became the prime suspect; in point of fact he was the only suspect identified by name on the day of the murder. When Sheriff Vosburg returned to the city that afternoon, he found many in Kalamazoo calling for Bill's arrest, which left the sheriff with the not so small matter of locating him.

Two pugilists square off in front of the Kalamazoo College men's dormitory c1877.
From the collection of the Kalamazoo Public Library

CHAPTER 8:

Solemnity of the Sabbath
-Broken by a Prize Fight

Kalamazoo Gazette, December 17, 1875

O N SUNDAY DECEMBER 12th, 1875, the congregation of the small chapel found in Texas Township gathered for fellowship. Disrupting those endeavors was a man going by the name Slingman, who was not well known to those present and rumored to be from Buffalo, who had designs on agitation. It seems Slingman fancied himself a pugilist and began to create quite a stir during the proceedings of the day with his verbosity taking the form of a challenge to any and all present should they like to test his fighting prowess. After suffering this man's boorish behavior for far too long a number of those present set young William Downey with the task of silencing the braggart. Being made of indissoluble nerve and physicality to match, William agreed to Slingman's terms in an effort to remove the man for the good of the congregation. With their respective entourages in tow, Downey and Slingman made their way to Eagle Lake where they procured a number of boats and rowed out to the island. There, on the normally tranquil bank, William engaged Slingman in thirty rounds of bare-knuckle fighting. Now, if you believe the initial accounts of the contest it was William who received the worst of it, but there is some indication that it was the entourages of both fighters who, upon seeing the bruised and bloodied faces of the combatants, decided the fighting should be ended before serious damage was done. Regardless of who more emphatically rang whose bell, both men were quickly made aware that their most un-Sabbath-like activities had not gone over with members of the moralistic local public. With the sheriff having been alerted to their activities young Downey and Slingman fled, presumably in different directions. Within days Officer Brownell had tracked William to Grand Rapids and promptly returned him to Kalamazoo to face Judge Allen. For his part in the disturbance William was given a $20 fine, which he promptly paid.

In the short time that the two young men had been on the run all manner of stories had circulated in the papers regarding the fight, with some quick to blame young William. But, as is frequently the case, expeditious reporting often takes precedence over the truth. Upon his return to town William's explanation of the day's events was found satisfactorily credible to publish in the *Gazette*, which then posited that William should have been more freely allowed to give Slingman a good pounding. With his fine paid, and his good name relatively unscathed, William's short spell as an individual on the wrong side of the law was ended.

For anyone still hesitant to believe William's account of the affair it is worth noting that Slingman failed to pay the $20 fine levied against him. When he was then summarily arrested by Officer Brownell for failure to make restitution, Slingman demonstrated his displeasure by attempting to engage the officer in fisticuffs in the same manner as he had William. Officer Brownell quickly corrected Slingman's mistake ... and he was led to his new accommodation in the county jail, his true character exposed.

An officer goes about his business on the northwest corner of Main and Burdick Streets c1890.

From the collection of the Kalamazoo Public Library

68

CHAPTER 9:
A Farmer Plain and Simple

Kalamazoo Gazette on Sheriff Vosburg
October 21, 1894

WHILE IT WOULD be unfair to deny that William Vosburg was a well-intentioned man, few would argue that he was not ill-equipped to deal with the challenge he soon faced as the newly elected Sheriff of Kalamazoo. Only three months removed from his life as a farmer, William Vosburg had not only been a surprising victor over the incumbent Sheriff William Downey but had also been an unlikely candidate as his own party's nominee. When the county's Republican convention was held in September 1892 and the first ballot was counted, it was former sheriff John Dix who received the majority of the votes, with William Vosburg finishing second to last among the original five nominees. Although it appeared likely that Dix would take the nomination, a consensus had not been reached during the first ballot. In an effort to achieve a majority decision nine subsequent ballots were taken with William Vosburg not finishing higher than fourth in any of them. When the eleventh ballot was taken, William Vosburg's fortunes brightened somewhat, but he still only managed just over half the number of votes that Dix received. It appeared John Dix's nomination was imminent, but as the twelfth ballot was prepared a curious accusation was made. Someone had noticed that a man who was not a delegate had been voting for Dix; it was then announced that the ballots were being "stuffed" in John Dix' favor. This resulted in great turmoil, and a general wave of support poured in the direction of William Vosburg at the expense of the former sheriff. When the twelfth ballot was taken, it was the underdog William Vosburg who secured the most votes. Realizing that he had lost nearly all support John Dix withdrew his name from the race. With only three individuals left in the running the final ballot was taken, and William Vosburg secured the nomination. Just over a month later, riding a wave of Republican support, which coincided with the presidential election,[3] William Vosburg narrowly defeated William Downey to become the sheriff of Kalamazoo.

William Vosburg would begin his tenure as sheriff in January of 1893 with sixteen prisoners already housed in the county jail. Although arrests were made by the sheriff's department within the first few months of the Vosburg administration, the majority of those added to the jail rolls were drunks or vagrants. While police work of this kind was rightly valued and expected there were growing concerns within Kalamazoo as the perpetrators of a number of recent crimes, which were seen as being of a serious nature, had yet to be identified or apprehended. One Kalamazoo citizen summed up his frustrations thusly in January of 1893: "I cannot remember when the police made a capture of a thief who stole anything unless he stole it for the express purpose of getting caught."

Given the bold nature of the following incidences it appears

---

3 Democrat Grover Cleveland won the 1892 presidential election, but the majority of Kalamazoo supported the incumbent, Republican President Benjamin Harrison. This support was undoubtedly bolstered by the strong Harrison family connection within Kalamazoo as Judge Bazel Harrison had been one of the first settlers to the county and remains one of the most prominent of Kalamazoo's founders. Judge Harrison was a cousin of former president William Henry Harrison, whose grandson Benjamin was favored by Kalamazoo in the 1892 election.

that this gentleman's grumblings may not have been unwarranted; and given what we now know about Louis Schilling's horrific death it is worth considering if the murderer was active in Kalamazoo during the first few months of the Vosburg administration.

On the morning of January 20th, local architect H.B. Flagler woke in his house at 905 West Main St. to find that someone had entered his home during the night and disturbed a number of items of clothing. After searching his property Mr. Flagler found that his overcoat had been removed from the house and was lying in the front yard, not far from his empty pocketbook. Having drawn $80 from the bank the previous day it appears that the thief or thieves had entered his home with the specific intent of locating his pocketbook as there were a number of other valuable items near the overcoat that were not molested. While Mr. Flagler's estranged wife suspected the story to be a fabrication, Flagler was adamant that he'd been robbed, and no further developments in the case were made.

On January 24th, near 7:30 p.m., Jacob Coleman, who lived alone on a small farm on Cork St. just east of Portage St., heard a rap at his door. Answering, Mr. Coleman found himself face-to-face with two masked men, one large and one small. The larger of the two men forcefully shoved a revolver in Mr. Coleman's face and demanded money before knocking him to the ground. As he lay prostrate in his doorway Mr. Coleman yelled, "Murder!" at the top of his lungs. Losing their nerve the two men made their escape through the woods. Although Sheriff Vosburg was notified, and the two would-be robbers' tracks were followed a significant distance, no positive identification was ever made. It was later made public that Mr. Coleman had received a substantial amount of money from the old country not long before the incident.

As the number of unsolved cases continued to grow, so did the grievances of the community. "There is now no doubt, in fact the evidence is conclusive, that the city is infested with sneak thieves whom the police and other officers are not acquainted with."[4]

On March 4th, Mr. C.H. Stevens of Grand Rapids, having missed his train, spent an evening in downtown Kalamazoo playing billiards and cribbage. Ending the night at Richmond's Restaurant Mr. Stevens enjoyed a slice of pie and a cup of coffee before heading to the Kalamazoo House. As he entered the alley just west of the inn, two men seized Mr. Stevens and covered his face with some cotton batting that may have been soaked in chloroform. As Mr. Stevens struggled to free himself from their grasp one of the men slashed him across the back of the hand. Fearing for his life Mr. Stevens relented, and the two men relieved him of his watch and a pocketbook containing $350. After the thieves made their getaway, and he'd regained his composure, Mr. Stevens went in search of an officer, quickly locating Patrolman Todd at Culver's Restaurant. When the police searched the reported scene of the crime, they found traces of blood on the ground and a sharp bit of tin with blood on it. It was later reported that Mr. Stevens had been in Kalamazoo a few weeks prior and had at that time carelessly flaunted a great deal of cash. Some speculated that he was identified as a "mark" at this time, while others alleged that Mr. Stevens had lost his money gambling and had staged the attack in order to avoid his wife's scorn. However, the evidence found at the crime scene lent credibility to Mr. Stevens' story, and suspicion was directed at two unnamed young men who seldom worked but were seen with money in the days following the robbery.

To the chagrin of many, the attitudes of at least a portion

4 *Kalamazoo Gazette*, January 28, 1893

of the officers in Kalamazoo did not correspond with the concerns of many regarding the ever-growing list of audacious crimes, as made evident by the following quote from an unnamed patrolman in March 1893: "More than half the reported robberies are fakes and they work to the detriment of the police department. There has been a number of cases within a few months which in the opinion of many amount to nothing."

Just three weeks later there would be no ambiguity regarding the validity of the reported offense. The first recorded murder in the city's history had taken place, and it was the responsibility of William Vosburg, and his son Edwin whom he had named under-sheriff, to lead the investigation. Unfortunately, given his very short tenure, Sheriff Vosburg returned to Kalamazoo a few hours after the murder with a very limited number of experiences on which he could rely for proven methods. Complaints would later be made that evidence had been neglected and standard protocol such as watching departing trains was ignored. To the chagrin of many Sheriff Vosburg also declined to deputize the much more experienced William S. Downey, even after a petition had been circulated and numerously signed by many Kalamazoo residents requesting that he do so. In fact, it was reported that no extra police were pressed into service at all following the murder. Although hubris and a lack of experience may have led Sheriff Vosburg to make some mistakes in the execution of the investigation, he was not unmotivated. With reports flying in and the case rife with confusion the efforts of the sheriff's department focused on three main areas during the first day of the investigation.

Their first, and their seemingly chief, priority was to locate the man that Mrs. Whitcomb had seen hurrying past her home moments after the murder. In order to accomplish this task Sheriff Vosburg flooded neighboring counties with the following notice:

> "Five hundred dollar reward for the arrest and conviction of the murderer of Louis Schilling at Kalamazoo at noon on March 21, 1893. Suspect an unknown man; short, heavy built, dressed rather poorly in light clothes, probably wore short beard and had a very red face. I will give $500 on conviction of the murderer, for the arrest in any jail in the United States."

There was also the matter of Bill White, who many in Kalamazoo considered the likely murderer. As officers searched the city, and inquiries were made regarding Bill's activities on the day of the murder, the sheriff discovered that he had been seen in the city around 4 p.m. that same afternoon. Those who claimed to have seen Bill also claimed that, rather than blood, his boots were covered in black mud. Although multiple people had observed him in the city, officers were unable to locate Bill, and he reportedly fled for a second time around 10 p.m. that night.

Unable to locate the red-faced man or Bill, the sheriff's department rather frenziedly began to scour the city for anyone they deemed suspicious. Three tramps that fit this criterion were found hiding under a lumber car at the depot late that first evening. With no evidence or indication that the men had been involved with the murder they were soon released. The first day of the investigation would come to a close with Sheriff Vosburg pursuing a number of leads but having made no findings of note.

Looking east down Main towards Portage Street c1877.
From the collection of the Kalamazoo Public Library

CHAPTER 10:
The Pruning Hook Murder
Jackson Citizen Patriot, May 07, 1877

S OME FOUR MILES south of town in the Kilgore brothers' woods John Hewitt lay on the ground bleeding profusely from his head. Standing over the wounded man, Dan Van Wagoner took aim with his revolver and fired four times into John Hewitt's chest. Dan then removed $190 from John Hewett's pocket, mounted his buggy, and returned to town.

Canadian John Hewitt was nearly forty years of age and by all accounts an agreeable man undeserving of the ordeal in which Dan Van Wagoner entangled him. The two had originally met on April 23rd 1877 as they traveled by train from Ionia to Grand Rapids. As they passed the time engaged in friendly conversation John Hewitt explained to Dan that he was a patent right agent on his way to Kalamazoo in search of business opportunities. As luck would have it, explained Dan, he, too, was in the patent business and was pursuing a number of potentially profitable new inventions with startup capital being his only obstacle. John Hewitt agreed to lend Dan a small amount of money and accepted his revolver as collateral with the understanding that the two would share in potential future profits. Parting ways in Grand Rapids John Hewitt boarded a train for Kalamazoo, while Dan Van Wagoner continued on to his original intended destination of Chicago. Although he'd conned John Hewitt out of a small sum Dan could not stop thinking about the larger pool of cash from whence his "loan" had come. He soon decided that John Hewitt was too tempting a target to let out of his grasp, and upon his arrival in Chicago he almost immediately boarded a Kalamazoo-bound train. Arriving on the evening of the 24th of April Dan checked into the Burdick Hotel. The following morning, he dressed and set out to find and murder John Hewitt.

By noon the two "partners" were headed south out of town in a carriage that Dan had rented from Col. Waddle. The purported purpose of their excursion was to collect branches with which to demonstrate the pruning shears that Dan Van Wagoner claimed as his innovative creation. As they approached Portage Township the two men encountered Henry Turner who was on his way to Bochove's Grocery. Being unfamiliar with Kalamazoo Dan inquired where they could find some timber, and Henry directed them to a spot near the Woodburry Mill. The men thanked Henry and proceeded to follow his directions until they located a spot they found satisfactory. Continuing a short distance from the road into the woods the two men began to collect their props. In a moment that highlights both his trusting nature and naiveté, John Hewitt handed Dan Van Wagoner his gun when the later exclaimed that he wished to use it to shoot a blue jay that had alighted upon a nearby tree. With gun in hand, and greed clogging the cockles of his heart, Dan exclaimed, "Look over there!" Falling for what must have been a cliché trick even in 1877 John Hewitt turned and was promptly struck in the head by the pruning shears. As he lay dazed on the ground he was struck once more with the shears before Dan Van Wagoner stepped over him, gun in hand.

The money he'd taken from John Hewitt certainly seemed an easy enough bit of work. Much easier than some of the legitimate means he'd attempted and failed at in the past. When Dan returned to the Wattles' barn with the team of horses he'd rented, he cheekily joked about being "lucky" in collecting a hundred or two dollars that day. Visibly pleased with himself, and flush with cash, Dan Van Wagoner then set out on the town to do a bit of shopping in an effort to improve his toilet. As he perused the shops of downtown Kalamazoo Dan possessed the nonchalance of a man with no fear of his victim being discovered. He made no attempt to go unnoticed and even regaled a number of individuals he met with fanciful stories about being a detective on the trail of a known forger (he was himself a sometime-forger). While in this frame of mind, it must then have come as quite a shock to him when, while shopping for a hat at Denton's, Officer Jennings approached him.

Waking as if from an afternoon slumber John Hewitt found himself in considerable discomfort. A mental fog hung heavy about his faculties with his mind telling him almost nothing about how he had reached his present state of duress. Bleeding profusely from his head and chest and unable to stand, he began to crawl in the direction that he believed he had come from. Taking a step when able, but moving on his hands and knees the majority of the way, John Hewitt dragged himself roughly 1/8 of a mile to the nearest road. With his life fading the sound of an approaching horse caught his ear, and he cried out in desperation, "For God's sake, help me, I'm killed; I think I am dying!" The man on the approaching horse just happened to be Henry Turner, the same man who had given John and Dan directions earlier in the day. Acting quickly Henry acquired assistance, and the grievously injured man was brought to the home of George Turner, Henry's father. Sheriff Gates was then notified and together with Henry Turner began to provide local officials and businesspersons with a description of the man seen in the company of John Hewitt earlier in the day. As previously mentioned, Dan Van Wagoner's garrulous ways had made his presence in town well known. In almost no time at all a local gentleman spotted the wanted stranger and alerted the police.

Coolly cleaning his nails using a knife he'd borrowed from the turnkey, Dan Van Wagoner hardly seemed like a person caught dead to rights for attempted murder. Although he'd initially told officers that his surname was Strong, he soon relented and mustered almost no defense at all. Even if he had protested there was little doubt as to his guilt. When apprehended, officers searched him and found a revolver with four spent casings, about $150 in cash, and a notebook previously belonging to John Hewitt. He was also brought to John Hewitt's bedside and recognized by the victim as well as Henry Turner and Col. Wattles, who identified him as the man they had seen in the company of Hewitt directly before the attack. With no need to further build a case against the accused, Dan was brought before Justice Allen the day after his arrest. When asked if he wished to make a statement, he replied that he desired to be sentenced immediately as he had thought that John Hewitt was dead and could not stand to be in his presence again. After a short discussion between the sheriff and the prosecuting attorney Dan was informed that sentencing would take place that same afternoon. Satisfied that he would never again have to face his victim, Dan Van Wagoner made a full confession.

Although he was forthcoming regarding his crimes against John Hewitt, Dan was hesitant to divulge information on one subject, his background. This information had to be sleuthed out by Deputy Sheriff Allen who tracked the defendant's activities to Muskegon. There he learned that Dan Van Wagoner came from a respected and successful family. His father was a wealthy farmer near Milwaukee who had financed Dan's higher education and had even given him startup capital to enter the business world. It was also learned that Dan had a reputation for cruelty and had given his parents considerable trouble over the years. With little doubt regarding the facts of the case, or Dan Van Wagoner's character, he was expediently sentenced to 45 years in Jackson Prison.

On the morning of May 6, 1877 an immense crowd gathered at the Michigan Central depot to see Dan Van Wagoner off. As he waited on the platform in shackles, he casually smoked a cigar while engaging those who wished to do so in conversation. He claimed to be accepting of the sentence given him but was of the opinion that if Hewitt survived, 25 years was a more fitting sentence. To one *Gazette* reporter who approached him for comment Dan Van Wagoner claimed to have recently had a female visitor at the jail who'd slipped him a note in order to let him know that a band of armed desperadoes were on their way from Chicago with the express purpose of breaking him out. He also claimed that if one searched the stove of his hotel room at the Burdick Hotel they would find the burned remains of some $500 in "queer" greenbacks, which he had decided not to "press" following his acquisition of other funds. As the train pulled out of the station the crowd cheered, happy to be rid of the man.

A few days after he was sent up, Dan Van Wagoner's father arrived in Kalamazoo. He'd recently been in Texas and had heard nothing of the ordeal until he returned to the Midwest and read about his son's activities in the Chicago papers. Arriving too late to see his son Mr. Van Wagoner took the opportunity to witness Dan's handiwork. Col. Wattles brought Mr. Van Wagoner to the home of George Turner where John Hewitt was recuperating. It was said that upon seeing John Hewitt's badly cut up condition Mr. Van Wagoner became quite emotional. And yet, curiously, he almost immediately began to fight to minimize the punishment Dan received. It wasn't long before strings were pulled in order to get Dan transferred to Ionia where he could be closer to friends and family. By early 1878, it was reported that Dan's cell rivaled the comforts of many a respected home: with a new spring bed, upholstered chairs, pictures on the walls, and Brussels carpets on the floors. Great effort was also expended to secure Dan a pardon. This initially proved difficult, perhaps owing to then Governor Croswell's efforts to reduce bribery and corruption. Undismayed, the friends of Dan Van Wagoner continued to plot other avenues of his release.

During the week of November 16th 1878, a man and a woman arrived at the Ionia Hotel. The man gave his name as D. Goble of Dubuque, Iowa, while the woman was known as "Mrs. Ely". It was quickly realized that the two were relatives of Dan (although it was unknown at the time they were in fact Dan's sister and her dentist husband) who had come to petition for his release, among other things. On the evening of November 18th, Mrs. Ely visited Dan at the prison. A few hours after the visit, Dan escaped. How he had managed this feat was unknown at the time, but both D. Goble and Mrs. Ely were arrested. A keeper at the prison was also suspected of aiding Dan and was quickly "let go". With members of his family held on suspicion, and a reward of $300 posted for his return, Dan Van Wagoner had seemingly vanished.

Months passed without so much as a sighting, and then, in a St. Louis paper, a surprising letter was published, the author of which was Dan Van Wagner. In this letter Dan made all kinds of stipulations to Warden Grafton of the Ionia State Prison should he turn himself in. Although the warden suspected that the letter was simply a ploy to alert Dan's friends to his whereabouts, it was hoped that he may consider turning himself in to clear his family members who were still facing charges related to his escape. Apprehensively Warden Grafton published his own letter assuring Dan that he would not be mistreated should he turn himself in; somewhat unsurprisingly, there was no response.

Additional months passed, and it wasn't until March of 1879 that Warden Grafton would receive another curious communiqué, this time from Hamilton, Ontario. The author was listed as a detective named C.E. Randall who claimed that he had Dan Van Wagoner in custody. Although Warden Grafton immediately had his suspicions he had few options other than to play along. Responding, Warden Grafton let detective Randall know that he and the reward money were headed east in order to take custody of Dan. When the warden arrived in Detroit, he received another series of curious dispatches. The first read, "Shall start on next train. Prisoner drugged," followed quickly by a dispatch stating that the "detective" lacked the $5 to purchase train tickets with which to bring Dan to Detroit. With all doubt removed Warden Grafton wired Dan Van Wagoner $5. A few hours later, he received a telegraph from Niagara Falls, which read, "Have beat C.E.R., do not expect reward. Meet me here tonight. Stop at America House." Signed D.V.W.

Laughing, Warden Grafton remarked, "Yes, he's beaten C.E.R., and he's beaten me out of $5."

For his part Dan Van Wagoner seemed to realize that his detective pretense was over and soon sent a dispatch requesting that Warden Grafton meet him in Clifton, Ontario where he intended to turn himself in. Knowing the character of the man Warden Grafton theorized that Dan Van Wagoner was planning to lure him to a meeting and "lay him out" in order to steal the $300 reward. As backup, Warden Grafton enlisted the assistance of Patrolman Michael Coleman, and together the two traveled to Buffalo, NY. There Warden Grafton also enlisted the assistance of Detective Tom Curtin, one of the best men in the Buffalo force. These American officers then crossed the border and coordinated with the Canadian officers of Clifton, Ont. As he had thoroughly overplayed his hand the team of experienced lawmen quickly found Dan and apprehended him without incident. Detective Curtin would later remark that Dan was "in" with a very bad gang of crooks and stated, "There is no doubt in my mind that he intended to croak Grafton. He told me that when the trains were in the depot he had only to whistle to call up a dozen friends."

After five months on the run many questions remained regarding Dan's escape and whereabouts during his absence. As he always was, Dan was downright giddy to talk about himself; although he took considerable pains to steer suspicion away from his family. According to Dan the escape was facilitated by the night-keeper, Henry W. Nay, who it was claimed was paid $11,000 for his assistance (how Dan expected anyone to believe he'd raised $11,000 without his parents' help beggars belief). According to Dan, on the night of the 18th of November, shortly after his sister's visit, night-keeper Nay had instructed him to fashion a makeshift body in his bed using books and a quilt. Dan was then ushered upstairs and secreted away in an empty cell. The plan took an unexpected turn when another night-keeper who was making his rounds unwittingly locked the cell Dan was hiding in. When Nay discovered Dan locked in, he began to rethink the entire enterprise. Dan claimed that at this point in the escape he was forced to motivate the night-keeper into action through the use of two revolvers, which he claimed he'd paid $20 to another keeper to smuggle in to him. With Nay coaxed into action the brake was pulled and the lock released. Descending one flight of stairs Dan then went out a window and made his escape via a rope normally used to draw up coal and water. He'd then made his way to Chicago where he'd donned a bald cap and sectional whiskers. Over the next five months he claimed to have fashioned all kinds of outlandish disguises for himself while he traveled to Texas, Havana, Jamaica, and eventually Canada.

Unsurprisingly, efforts to free Dan Van Wagoner did not cease, and in November 1882, he escaped again. The particulars unknown, it appears that he faked a religious conversion in order to gain some liberties from the prison guards. He then took advantage of these newfound freedoms to escape the prison. Although the manufacture of his escape was ambiguous, the Van Wagoner family dynamic was well understood. Deputy Perry, who'd been tasked with recapturing Dan, immediately traveled to Wisconsin in order to shadow the Van Wagoners. No member of the family was allowed to move without the eye of a detective upon them, and within days Mr. Van Wagoner was observed sending a package to a "D. Mills" in Holland, MI (Dan's middle name was Mills). The next morning, in Holland, MI, shortly after the express office opened, a man stepped to the counter to inquire about said package. Stepping out from a concealed location Deputy Perry slipped a handcuff on Dan's wrist.

Although it was no secret that Dan's family had long been pressing for a pardon, the unanimous response from those in Kalamazoo was predictable outrage when they read the following headline:

"Governor Begole this morning granted pardons and commuted the sentence of four convicts. Among the latter is the notorious Dan Van Wagoner, sent to Jackson Prison from Kalamazoo County, May 5, 1877, on a sentence of forty-five years for assault with intent to murder. Van Wagoner's relatives are very wealthy, and have been persistent in their efforts to get him out." December 18, 1884

On behalf of the people of Kalamazoo former Sheriff Gates wrote a letter to the governor reminding him of the particularly cold and calculated crimes that Dan had previously committed. Former Governor Jerome called the decision to pardon Dan an "outrage" saying he "had no interest in seeing Van Wagoner free to join the band of robbers and murderers to which he formerly belonged." The negative and energetic response was so great that Governor Begole felt compelled to personally write a letter to the *Evening News* defending his decision. This letter is so factually inaccurate and dishonest it is hard not to draw conclusions regarding the character of Governor Begole, but I will let his own reasoning make the case.

"The 'notorious' Dan Van Wagoner, as he is called, never killed any one. I am not posted fully in regard to his crime, nor have I had any formal petitions for his release. What I know of him is my acquaintance with him and his prison record, which has always been of the best. He once made a break for liberty, was soon recaptured and has always been one of the most faithful, hard-working men in prison. His sentence was most excessive. He was first sentenced for twenty-years, and then, for an impertinent remark, the judge added twenty-five years more to his time. For nearly a year and a half I had resolved to commute his sentence to twenty years, and should have done that now had I believed, from my own knowledge of his health, that he could live half of the balance of 20 years. I have commuted his sentence to one year from the first of January next. This is as long as I believe he can live.

Josiah W. Begole, Governor. Otter Lake, Mich., Dec 25. 1885"

Defying the wishes of many, Governor Begole had Daniel "Dan" Van Wagoner released. Contrary to what the governor anticipated, Dan died forty years later in San Francisco, CA.

The widow Schilling stands with her grandchildren and youngest daughter Grace (far right) in front of the Schilling family home at 329 Portage c1894. *From the collection of the Kalamazoo Valley Museum*

CHAPTER 11:
Suspect in Jail – Murderer at Large
Kalamazoo Telegraph, March 22, 1893

T WO DAYS AFTER the murder, as the Schilling family prepared for Louis's funeral they received a knock on their front door. Answering, the family was greeted by a somewhat excitable stranger who introduced himself as C.B. Peterson. The arrival of well-wishers was not unexpected but the rather peculiar request of C.B. Peterson to view the corpse of Mr. Schilling was. When C.B. was instructed to return on the 25th when the scheduled viewing was to take place, he insisted that he must view the body that same day as he was soon to leave the area. Surprisingly, his request was granted, and he was led to the room where the body of Louis Schilling was lying in wait for burial. After viewing the corpse to his satisfaction C.B. was led to the front door. The Schilling family then watched as the strange man stepped to the front walkway and took off at a run northward towards South St. Thinking the entire incident odd the Schillings reported C.B. Peterson to the sheriff's department, and later that day Officer Merrell located and brought him to jail.

The apprehension of C.B. Peterson was just the latest in a growing list of inquiries that local officers had made in the days following the murder. After Mrs. Whitcomb's report of the red-faced man was made public, four additional women had come forward to say that they too had seen a similar looking man on Portage St. near 1 p.m. on the day of the murder. Based on their descriptions, which varied slightly regarding the man having a red or a deathly pale face, a number of local men were brought in under suspicion. One of these men was a local string butcher named Tame Colligan who'd had frequent run-ins with the law over the years, which included charges of stealing sheep and multiple arrests for assault and battery. A local scavenger named Charles Hatch was also detained as he somewhat fit the description the ladies had provided and had reportedly worked for a man who'd had problems with Louis Schilling. When the pair of men was presented before the witnesses, it was unequivocally decided that neither was the man the women had seen. Officers also conducted a parallel series of inquiries in order to locate a livery rig seen leaving the city directly after the murder and which individuals living south of the city had seen speeding through the countryside. This inquiry too soon turned fruitless when it was discovered that the driver of the buggy was a friend of the Schilling family who had rented the rig in order to ride to the home of Louis's cousin in Pavilion Township in order to notify him of the ordeal.

Of the numerous suspects questioned within the first few days of the investigation there was only one man who was detained for any significant amount of time. Described as a laborer, William Thompson was in actuality more of a vagrant who had a penchant for peculiar behavior and lies. Shortly after the Louis Schilling affair became known, multiple people living on South St. reported that Thompson had knocked on their respective front doors within an hour of the murder. Equipped with a letter that in part described his struggles as a deaf mute and his desire to provide for his motherless children currently in the care of his sister, who it was claimed lived in the area, Thompson had been looking for a handout. After his activities were reported Deputy Sheriff Merrill conducted a short search and located Thompson on the morning of the 22nd. When arrested, Thomson pretended not to understand the officers and persisted in his act as a deaf mute. It was soon determined that not only was his implied malady an act, but he had no children and was unknown at the address he had listed as his sister's. William Thompson was most certainly a charlatan, but there was very little to implicate him in the Schilling murder. However, after Thompson was apprehended it was noted that he appeared to be wearing different clothing than what he'd reportedly worn on the day of the murder. This small mystery was enough for the sheriff to keep Thompson in custody pending further investigation. In reality Thompson appears to have been little more than an eccentric character that was easily locatable in the absence of the man most favored as the culprit, Bill White.

Kalamazoo's second courthouse c1893.
The jail is visible through the trees in the background on the left.
From the collection of the Kalamazoo Public Library

As officers attempted to unravel the truth from within William Thompson's bizarre statements the coroner's jury was conducting their inquiries in the office of Justice Wattles. As curious onlookers packed the halls of the county courthouse in an effort to glean new developments in the case it was soon realized that those called to testify were as baffled regarding the circumstances surrounding the murder as the members of the coroner's jury were themselves. The proceedings began with a brief discussion of the murder weapon. It had initially been Dr. Ostrander's opinion that the slashes that had nearly severed Louis Schilling's head from his body had not been inflicted with a knife unless it was a very dull one. When called to testify, Dr. Bosman stated that while the wounds to Louis's neck appeared jagged, this was not indicative of a dull weapon, and his examination led him to believe that a knife had been the murder weapon. With scant other avenues of inquiry to pursue Bill White then became the primary focus of the inquisition. Curiously, the first bit of testimony regarding Bill White came from Louis Schilling's son Gus who testified that he had encountered Bill at 7 a.m. near the Kalamazoo House on the morning of the murder. The two had briefly spoken to each other, and Gus claimed to have given Bill a black stiff hat before the two carried on their separate ways. A man named James Bailey then testified that he too had seen Bill the previous morning between 10:30 and 11:00 as the latter passed by the Burdick Street window. Charles Raymond, who had moved furniture for Bill White in the past, testified that he "thought" he saw Bill and a man he described as having "yellow" skin on Portage St. between 11:30 and 12:30. The "yellow" man was wearing a brown overcoat and a soft black cap and had chin whiskers. Walter Schilling would later testify that he had seen a man who very closely matched this description lingering on the walk in front of the Schilling Market as he left for dinner a half hour before the murder. Walter explained that this man was looking in the Schilling Market window and was still there when Walter turned to look back as he reached South St. The last in the timeline to reportedly see Bill White before the murder was W.R. Holt who claimed that he had seen Bill White near 12:30 p.m. around the corner from the Schilling Market, in front of the City Barbershop on E. Main. Police officers and a *Gazette* reporter would later scrutinize this account when it was noted that Mr. Holt claimed that the man he'd seen was not particularly dark skinned, which Bill White was. When pressed, Mr. Holt stated that the man he had seen was one of the men that had struck another with a board a few years before. This information led many to believe that W.R. Holt had actually seen John Hopkins with whom Bill White had been convicted of assault in 1891.

Given the testimony heard at the coroner's inquest it seemed that not only had Bill White suspiciously fled the city after the murder but also that he and another man had been in the area of the Schilling Market shortly before the murder took place. A much more dubious report had even begun to circulate that a man and woman had seen Bill leaving the alley in the rear of the market around the time of the murder. Although there were some questions as to the accuracy of both the identification and times surrounding these sightings, specifically the last one mentioned, the sheer number of people who had seen him, and the seemingly implausible coincidence that he would flee the city moments after the murder, solidified in the minds of many Bill's involvement in the crime. But Bill was not without friends, and wherever he was hiding he soon owed George Tyson a hefty thank you.

George Tyson was the younger brother of coroner's jury member and respected meat market owner Herbert Tyson. Unlike his upstanding older brother Herbert, George was a chronic drunk who was arrested so often that his wife had previously brought charges against a number of local bartenders in an effort to stop them serving her husband. At the time that Louis was murdered, George Tyson did his butchering at the Brooks' slaughterhouse, which counted Louis Schilling among their customers. The Brooks' slaughterhouse was a place where over the years "missing" livestock had turned up and where string butchers who were perhaps not welcome elsewhere could work. Bill White would likely have fallen into this category owing to his previously mentioned habit of stealing from his employers. Bill White had even been caught stealing from George Tyson in 1892, but regardless of this previous slight George was willing to testify on Bill's behalf. With the quotes differing somewhat it was reported that, when questioned, George Tyson had stated that Bill White had been at the slaughterhouse with him from 10 a.m. to between 2 and 3 p.m. George further claimed that Bill White had left town due to an argument over stolen property.

"I accused him of stealing tallow of me and said Id have him arrested. He begged off and agreed to pay for the tallow. I have not seen White since."

The following day, it was reported that Mr. Brooks (whether this was Granville or Charles is unknown) corroborated George Tysons's claim and stated that Bill White was at the slaughterhouse from "about 10:30 to not far from 2 o'clock." Although their statements regarding the timeframe that Bill was present at the slaughterhouse vary by one half to one full hour, the statements by George Tyson and Mr. Brooks directly contradict the testimony of those who claimed to see Bill White on the day of the murder. Not only do these statements call into question the sightings of Bill near the corner of Main and Portage Streets, but they would also seem to imply that both Patrolman Todd and Patrick Flynn had been incorrect in their estimation of the time that they had seen Bill moving west on the tracks.

With an alibi in place there were still a number of incongruities that made little sense when Bill White's words and actions were analyzed. Would he flee the city over a relatively small amount of stolen tallow? After all, he had stolen from his employers before. In fact, Bill had stolen two hundred and twenty pounds of tallow from his employer in 1889. For that offense he had only received a short stint in jail. He had also previously stolen from George Tyson and had received little more than a slap on the wrist. If Bill White did say that if he was captured he would be killed, it seems a gross overstatement based on the claimed circumstances. As time went on it became increasingly clear that locating Bill White was the only way to get to the bottom of these questions, but day after day he remained in the wind.

Back at the jail C.B. Peterson sat down with officers who quickly realized that his apprehension was just the latest in a long line of unproductive diversions. C.B. explained to officers that he had arrived in Kalamazoo earlier that week to do some advertising. On the day of the murder, he'd hired a number of local men to distribute fliers for him but had found himself short of the small change he needed to pay for their labor. In the pursuit of finding someone to break a quarter he had entered the Schilling Market shortly after noon. When C.B. later heard about the murder, he realized that he might have been one of the last to see the victim alive. Why C.B. Peterson would feel so compelled or entitled to satiate his curiosity by arriving unannounced to view a corpse is unknown, but it appears that is what he did. When asked why he had run away from the Schilling home so suspiciously after viewing the body, C.B. explained that as he departed it had begun to rain. Not wanting to get wet he'd set off quickly in order to mitigate the effects of the inclement weather.

A carriage leaves the Michigan Asylum for the Insane c1885.
From the collection of the Kalamazoo Valley Museum

CHAPTER 12:
Asylum

"The practice of dumping lunatics into Kalamazoo by officials in different parts of the state has been practiced for years. About one-fourth of the county patients at the asylum are this class"

Kalamazoo Gazette, February 06, 1893

I F ONE INSTITUTION from Kalamazoo's past both horrified while simultaneously meeting the rather morbid expectations of the local community it was the Michigan Asylum for the Insane. Since its opening in 1859 instances of misfortune involving the ill-fated inmates of the asylum were not uncommon. When contained within the walls of the hospital, these sordid events were often read in the local papers with curious pity. On the few occasions that the madness sometimes associated with the hospital threatened to bleed outside of its walls, the public were quick to voice their concerns.

Shortly past 3 a.m., Dr. Adams optimistically remarked that he had not lost strength and attempted to check his own pulse, finding it barely perceptible. No longer able to deny his hastily approaching death, Dr. Adams admitted to Drs. Wooster and Savage, who vigilantly attended to his final hours, that he felt sorry for his friends and relatives. Lying in his bed at the asylum, with his wounds dressed but inadequately mended, Dr. Adams slowly sank away, and just past 6 a.m. he was gone.

Described as kind and genial, Edward A. Adams was held in high regard by both colleagues and patients alike. Having grown up in Massachusetts Edward attended Amherst and then Buffalo Medical College. Originally moving to Kalamazoo as a temporary fill-in for vacationing physicians, Dr. Adams was soon recalled and made a permanent member of staff. Life at the asylum was described as being somewhat "shut off" from surrounding society, with colleagues and patients taking on numerous surrogate social roles in the daily lives of those who inhabited the hospital. In this capacity Dr. Adams was a significant and well-liked figure who was valued by nearly all who were fortunate enough to make his acquaintance. As a credit to both his character and competence Dr. Adams was named assistant superintendent in 1878.

Between 10:00 and 11:00 in the forenoon of January the 6th 1882, Dr. Adams had set out to conduct his daily rounds of the male department, of which he was in charge. Accompanied by Mr. Goodenough, the supervising attendant, Dr. Adams made a casual inspection of the north end of the transverse hall at the end of the north wing. Upon their return to the main hall they found the passage blocked by an agitated patient by the name of George Winans. Supposedly suffering from acute mania brought on by sunstroke the preceding summer, George Winans was a violent man. Having previously departed the asylum in the company of friends who falsely thought him well, Winans had quickly been returned in his now nearly permanent maniacal state. Seething about a letter he had written Winans demanded to know of Dr. Adams if it had been mailed. Even if the letter was not a nearly illiterate jumble of garbled thoughts folded up into what appeared to be a paper boat, which it was, the letter had in fact been handed to Dr.

Adams that very same morning. With no opportunity and possibly no intention of mailing the letter Dr. Adams replied that he had not in fact mailed the letter. Approaching from the doctor's right Winans yelled, "You didn't, eh!" and twice stabbed fiercely with a knife that he had concealed under his sleeve. One blow caught the doctor's coat and did no damage. The other blow saw the three-inch blade enter the doctor's abdomen a few inches below the breastbone and cut upwards making a gash as long as the wound was deep.

Initially falling to the ground Dr. Adams had pulled himself to his feet and run through the main hall, into the office building, and after calling for a doctor made his way up to his room. Meanwhile Winans carried on with his rampage and continued in his attempts to use the knife in a horrible fashion. Mr. Goodenough, and attendant William Hill, who had been mere feet away during the attack, eventually overcame the brute, with William Hill being stabbed fully in the thigh during the struggle. Dr. Hitchcock arrived shortly thereafter in order to dress Dr. Adams' wounds, but before long a hemorrhage was observed, and hope for the young doctor's recovery was all but lost.

It was later revealed that Winans had threatened Dr. Adams the week before the attack. This threat was considered serious enough to prompt a search of Winans' room, but no weapons were found in the possession of the deranged man at that time. Un-fortuitously it seems that just days after the search an attendant had momentarily sat on a settee in the north wing, and in doing so a bone-handled three-inch jack knife had fallen out of his pants and into a crevice. Winans apparently found the weapon, or another patient had found it and given it to him, and he had sharpened it on a stone windowsill for future use. Violating hospital policy the attendant had failed to report the knife when he realized it was missing, and thus a tragic set of events was set in motion that would see Dr. Adams become the last person murdered in the Village of Kalamazoo before the transition to city the following year.

Looking east down Main towards Portage St.
as workers lay streetcar tracks c1883.
From the collection of the Kalamazoo Valley Museum

After Dr. Adams was murdered, criticism regarding the supervision of violent patients at the asylum was robust and made all the more vociferous when Frank Cobb disappeared later that same year. Like Winans, Frank Cobb was a murderer, but, unlike Winans, Cobb had committed his crime before being committed. Growing up on a small farm a few hundred yards from the northwest shore of Eagle Lake in Texas Township Frank Cobb had always considered himself a "thinker". When he'd turned eighteen, Frank had enrolled in the agriculture college in Lansing but subsequently dropped out after just one year. He had then set out for the West Coast where he soon found himself committed to an asylum in Stockton, CA. When he was eventually considered well enough for release, Frank returned to Kalamazoo County and attempted to reintegrate into life on his father's farm. While he made a go of the "simple" life, it appears that Frank never lost some his more delusional intellectual pursuits. Later claiming that his younger brother Freddie had continually interrupted him while he was deep in thoughts that would have proved beneficial to the scientific world (it was also implied that that Freddie had caught Frank touching himself and teased him about it) Frank approached the breakfast table one morning and, grabbing twelve-year-old Freddie by the hair, pulled back his head and cut his throat from ear to ear. Nearly hysterical, Frank's seventeen-year-old sister, who had been sitting at the table during the attack, ran from the house to find help. When officials arrived at the Cobb farm, they found Frank working in the fields as if nothing had happened. Frank was initially decided to be competent enough to stand trial and was found guilty of his brother's murder.

Owing to his subsequent behavior while in jail, which included him smashing a chair over the head of cellmate Charles Warren, Frank was soon declared insane and transferred to the Kalamazoo Asylum. With little regard for the severity of his previous violent actions Frank was allowed to walk the grounds relatively unsupervised. In September of 1883, he slipped away from view and into a waiting carriage. Although some would later speculate that a ghostly figure scaring folks in the country west of Kalamazoo was Frank Cobb, he was never conclusively seen again.

The asylum wasn't just a dangerous place because of unstable inmates. At times it was the staff itself that posed the greatest threat to those within the hospital grounds. Just four months prior to Louis Schilling's murder a meat cutter and attendant at the asylum named Daniel Nevitt, which may have been an alias, admitted to kicking and stomping a patient named Konegan, whom he claimed had attacked him. Konegan had been found dead in his bed, and in response an inquisition had been initiated at the asylum. During the investigation Nevitt would claim that his confession, which had been made to a *Gazette* reporter while the two were drinking downtown, was false. Nevitt soon claimed that he had actually broken the ribs of a man named Thayer, who was still very much alive. During the subsequent investigation authorities at the asylum and Sheriff Downey were unable to ascertain if the injuries of the dead man were present when the patient had arrived from Jackson, MI three days prior to his death or if they were received while a patient at the asylum. No definitive conclusion was ever made, and although he was fired, Nevitt escaped further consequences for his role in what may have been the City of Kalamazoo's first murder.

Portrait of Louis Schilling in his middle age.
From the collection of the Kalamazoo Public Library

CHAPTER 13:
Eyes of the Dead Man

IN WHAT WAS described as a "forlorn hope" in 1888 the eyes of murder victim Mary Jane Kelly were photographed in London. Although thoroughly debunked in its scientific merits today, optography, as this process is known, presented desperate detectives and relations with the belief that the final dying visions of the deceased had been imprinted on their retinas. It was thought that these images could then be acquired by properly photographing the eyes. In the case of Mary Jane Kelly it was unrealistically believed that those images would supply detectives with the identity of her murderer, Jack the Ripper. Five years later, the proposal of acquiring clues in an otherwise vexing case remained an intriguing enough proposition that the eyes of Louis Schilling were likewise photographed. When the process failed to yield anything that would remotely be described as a clue, many were unsurprised. Still, there were some that argued that optography was not to blame, but rather it was that the process had been done incorrectly. These optography proponents theorized that the photographs were taken too quickly and should have been developed slowly as if one was photographing the moon or the night sky. In reality no alteration in the process of local photographer Thomas Wood would have yielded a superior result. Ultimately, the eyes of Louis Schilling would give up no more than those of the victims of the Ripper.

Louis Schilling was an unassuming man with few enemies; certainly no one to whom the finger of suspicion would instinctually point in the event of such tragedy. Born in Bavaria in 1833, Louis had immigrated to the United States in the 1860s. Pausing briefly in New York, he had then moved to Kalamazoo, where after years of hard work and respectable business he owned a fine home on Portage St. just a few blocks south of his meat market near the corner of Main and Portage Streets. Although he'd experienced the typical bickering common between a father and his eight children, there was little to suggest that any member Louis's family knew anything about his murder. With no known enemies or serious family squabbles simple greed seemed the likely motivation for Louis Schilling's attack. It was no secret that he often carried large amounts of cash, which he would use to purchase stock for his store. In the weeks prior to his death, a disagreement with a bank teller had resulted in Louis forgoing a number of deposits. This resulted in a temporarily larger amount of cash in his pocketbook than even he was accustomed to carrying. Owing to the desperate lengths the murderer had gone to in order to acquire Louis's pocketbook it is not unreasonable to assume that the culprit was aware of Louis's recent banking embargo and expected to acquire an uncommonly large score worthy of such an audacious crime. What the attacker appears not to have known was that Louis had resolved any temporary issues he'd had with his bank and had made two deposits totaling $240 in the week prior to his death. Those transactions meant that on the day that Louis Schilling was so desperately murdered his attacker ran from the market with a pocketbook that contained the rather modest sum of just $35.

While the lengths that someone had gone to in order to accomplish the task shocked many in Kalamazoo, the robbery itself was not entirely unsurprising to the Schilling family. For some time they had suspicioned that someone was planning to rob their home. Speaking to a *Gazette* reporter days after the murder, Walter Schilling revealed that in late October 1892, just before the first snowfall, the Schilling family dog had been found dead under a tree in the yard of their home. Initially it appeared as if the faithful companion had been shot, but upon closer inspection it seemed that someone had pierced the dog's side with something resembling the tong of a pitchfork. Forebodingly, whoever had stabbed the family pet had also then dispatched the animal by lacerating its throat. As a faithful companion to Louis the dog was said to bark dutifully at any disturbance, and the family felt that an unknown party had targeted the watchdog in preparation for an imminent burglary, never imagining that one of the family member's lives would be ended in a similar way.

As speculation and theories regarding the Schilling case continued to swirl there was a momentary sense of relief when, on March 25th, Sheriff Vosburg located Bill White working in a slaughterhouse in Lawton, MI. When arrested, Bill put up little resistance, and it was noted that the knife he was known to carry was nowhere to be found. When he was brought back to Kalamazoo and questioned, Bill explained his suspicious disappearance thusly: Just like his friends had stated, Bill claimed that he had been stealing tallow from George Tyson and had fled in order to avoid arrest for that crime. Bill also claimed that he'd already paid $1.50 of the $10 stolen and had agreed to pay off the rest. After a confrontation with George Tyson, during which George threatened to have him arrested, Bill claimed that he'd left the slaughterhouse, stopped to borrow $.10 to buy whiskey from Sam Polaski, and then headed out of town. With Bill's statement on record George Tyson and Mr. Brooks were re-interviewed, and both repeated their claim that Bill had been with them at the slaughterhouse from 10 a.m. to "not far from 2," with George re-corroborating the stolen tallow story. Although anomalies seemingly existed, the suspicion focused on Bill White ended abruptly following his retelling of the day's events, with the *Gazette* writing shortly thereafter, "The evidence against him lies totally in the imaginations of the people and there seems to be a strong tendency with many to talk about his whereabouts when they know nothing about him, and many do not even know him." This curious defense of the character of a man who had more than once threatened to kill people with a knife, had gravely assaulted at least one individual, and had stolen from every employer he'd ever had is somewhat puzzling, but following this report Bill White ceased to be discussed publically as a credible suspect.

Looking east down Main towards Portage Street c1890. *From the collection of the Kalamazoo Valley Museum*

CHAPTER 14:
Scaring Satan
-A Queer Michigan Sect

The Buffalo Enquirer, February 7, 1893

I N THE YEARS preceding the Schilling murder Kalamazoo was hardly what one would consider a regular topic of sensational national news coverage. The high profile crimes of the 1860s and '70s had long been forgotten, and local stories such as wild dogs roaming the streets and Mrs. Ella P. Chapman being hit by a train, flying twenty feet through the air, landing in a snow bank and then walking home as if nothing had happened were not dramatic enough to make print outside of southwest Michigan. The one story that had landed Kalamazoo within the pages of many a national paper in 1892 and 1893 was in fact incorrectly attributed and unfolded as follows.

In the Village of Coloma, some 40 miles west of the City of Kalamazoo, a crank named Thornton Carter had formed a sect called "The Church of Martyrdom". The "Carterites", as they came to be called, found flagellation a necessary devise in the pursuit of driving the devil from one's body, with members of the congregation working themselves into a fever as they beat the devil out of themselves and others. Horrified neighbors described hearing their cries and screams from as far as two miles away. Mr. Carter seemed especially supportive of such practices as long as he was the one dispensing the religious remedy.

Having beaten the devil out of his wife and a number of others Thornton Carter quickly exceeded the local citizens' capacity for religious eccentricity. In an effort to dissuade him from practicing his rather absurd version of piety in their backyards, a number of men intercepted him while he was driving home one evening. Thornton was then generously covered with tar and a handsome supply of chicken feathers. While this act did well to elevate the standing in the community of those involved in applying the tar, it did little to dissuade the Carterites from practicing their religious activities in Coloma.

By 1893, rumors of the Carterites' strange religious practices had become a sensation. It was reported that Thornton Carter, perhaps inspired by his own tarring ordeal, had ordered one woman, to whom it was said the evil one had cast an eye, to return home and encase herself in a coat of tar. Upstairs the woman's daughter was soon startled by screams of agony. Descending the stairs she found her mother engulfed in flames, the coat of tar having somehow been ignited. Having been proselytized to the point of stupidity, the daughter believed the flames to be a part of her mother's battle with the devil. Taking her own daughter with her the young mother walked to a neighbor's home nearly a quarter of a mile away to report the strange occurrence. The neighbors, not being Carterites, recognized the crisis and immediately rushed to the scene; what they observed was a grotesquery. In the yard they found the woman clinging to the clothesline post, her clothes completely burned from her body. Wherever she had grabbed the post, strips of flesh remained. After an hour of unimaginable suffering the old woman left this world.

Other dubious tales circulated amongst the national papers, but little legal action was taken against Thornton Carter; that was until numerous women were reported to have been impaired due to Thornton refusing them medical care.

In one instance, a woman of the Carter congregation fell from the edge of the mow to the barn floor below. In her pain the 60-year-old woman declared that her left side was paralyzed, which Carter deciphered to mean that they had the devil cornered in that particular debilitated part of her body. Under the direction of Thornton the congregation proceeded to drag and whip the woman about, which proved nearly fatal. In another instance of religious fervor Thornton Carter claimed that a second Christ was about to be born and tied the pregnant Mrs. Carter to a manger in the family barn. These negligent activities, along with Thornton Carter crippling a young girl with his wagon and then again withholding medical attention, eventually caused charges to be brought against him. While there was great support for punishment to be doled out using all available legal recourse, the courts found no charges with which they could hold Thornton to account.

Owing to proximity the Kalamazoo papers reported early and often on the strange proceedings in Coloma. In the somewhat antiquated age of news that was the late 19th century it was common for stories published in one paper to be reprinted around the country, sometimes abbreviated but often copied word for word. It was within this process that the lines of truth were crossed, and Kalamazoo was numerously listed as the home of Thornton Carter. Certainly Kalamazoo was no more pleased to be given this distinction than Berrien County was to be the actual home of the man (a fact local citizens reinforced when they once again applied the tar and feathers to Thornton in late 1893). Having recognized the error, one Kalamazoo supporter responded to the *Pittsburg Dispatch* thusly after an ill-informed reporter attempted to disparage Kalamazoo on the basis of her backwards citizenry.

"Kalamazoo is not only one of the handsomest cities in Michigan, but her citizens are, as a whole, liberal, cultivated, and progressive. It would be just as fair to pass upon the character of Pittsburg from the report of some escapade in Diamond Alley. Besides, the society to which the dispatch refers does not exist in Kalamazoo."

Somewhat surprisingly given the physical suffering so commonly endured by those around him, support for Thornton Carter remained strong within his small collective, exhibited at one point when his followers started carving his likeness onto silver coins. Living together on the Carter property with his family of twelve and thirty to forty followers, Thornton spent the rest of his life in relative obscurity until his passing in 1914.

Mugshot of Clem Blood taken in 1906.
Courtesy of The Zhang Collections Center- Western Michigan University

CHAPTER 15:
The Cranial Developments of Clem Blood

To those untrained in the "science" of phrenology Clem Blood's appearance disclosed little of his true character. The ignorant may even be forgiven for being impressed by some of the outward attributes of the man, but to a trained phrenologist Clem was an obvious criminal. Firstly, there was an observable imbalance within his mental organization, which resulted in the region responsible for moral sentiments being defective. His temporal lobes too appeared abnormal resulting in an individual of a selfish, thievish nature. His comparatively full occipital lobes caused Clem to seek partnerships with other people, which meant that a criminal like Clem surrounded himself with other morally deficient individuals. Once in the company of these potential cohorts Clem's dominant disposition, notably exhibited by the crown of his head, enabled him to persuade them into joining him in repugnant antisocial activities.

If this summarized analysis taken from the observations of a phrenologist seems impressive, perhaps even to the point of adding some validation to the debunked science of phrenology, it is worth noting that this examination was made in 1910 after Clem had already engaged in a well-publicized criminal career spanning two decades.

As thousands of mourners gathered for Louis's funeral at the Schilling home on March 26th, William Thompson remained in the county jail under suspicion. Although there was no evidence linking him to the crime, local officials were still hesitant to free the man. Making his prolonged incarceration even more unsatisfying was the new cellmate Thompson would soon receive, Clem Blood. In 1893, Clem was a young man but an old offender who, as he would throughout his life, exhibited a proclivity for violence that separated him from even the most well-known Kalamazoo criminals. Clem had had his first significant run-in with the law in 1889 when as a teenager he was charged with burglary and sent to the industrial school for boys in Lansing. Returning to Kalamazoo in 1891 Clem was again arrested for burglary. As he was by that time an adult he was given three years in Jackson State Prison. After serving roughly half of his sentence Clem was released and returned to Kalamazoo where he was arrested in January of 1893, this time for stealing an overcoat. Receiving thirty days in the county jail Clem was incarcerated for at least a portion of this time with Bill White, who was serving his thirty-day sentence for drunkenness. The crime that landed Clem in jail on March 26th was the midday burglary of William Osborn's house, which was north of Kalamazoo City in Cooper Township. Although Mr. Osborn was away at the time that his home was robbed, somehow someone from the Brooks' farm possessed information related to the case and called the sheriff's office with a tip. Officers quickly found Clem at his home where they also located the rifle, ammunition, razors, clothing, and other various provisions he had stolen. In addition to the items he had removed from the Osborn home it was reported that Clem had also taken time during the burglary to enjoy some milk and a slice of cherry pie. When apprehended, Clem made little effort to protest his innocence and expressed regret that the rifle he had acquired during the burglary was not more readily available during his arrest, as he would have liked "to do for" the officers who had caught him. With his conviction a mere formality Clem received three and a half years in prison, a sentence he would demonstrate his displeasure with by destroying his own clothing. After being supplied with a new suit at the public's expense Clem was soon off to Ionia.

Clem's focus on clothing seems to have been a specific peculiarity of his as he was arrested multiple times throughout his life for stealing clothing while also frequently destroying clothing in fits of anger and hysterics, something his cellmate could attest to as in their short period of incarceration together Clem had terrorized William Thompson by destroying his clothing as well. Although Thompson and many others in Kalamazoo were pleased when a Grand Rapids bound train departed Kalamazoo with Clem inside, if any suspected him of the Schilling murder it was never publicly implied. But, as will be further described, the most incriminating aspects of Clem Blood's criminal activities were yet to take place. A closer look at Clem's crimes suggests that not only did he deserve inclusion as a Schilling murder suspect, but his future actions suggest him one of the most capable criminals operating in Kalamazoo at that time.

Following his three-year stint in Ionia Clem returned to Kalamazoo in 1896 and, along with his brother Vern, was nearly immediately arrested for larceny. In an effort to avoid the workhouse the seldom-stable Clem downed a significant amount of opium, apparently hoping it would incapacitate him to the point of being unconvict-able. Unsuccessful in his attempt to avoid sentencing Clem was given thirty days at the workhouse.

A few months later, in January of 1897, local officers again wanted Clem and Vern, this time for the abuse and theft of sheep. With the pair's clandestine thieves' den on S. Burdick

St. a loosely guarded secret, Sheriff Snow made his way to the Bloods' front door and knocked. Answering, Vern Blood declared to the sheriff that he had no knowledge of his brother's whereabouts. Doubtful of Vern's claims Sheriff Snow ambled a few steps down the walk when he happened to turn and see Clem approaching. Immediately ordering Clem to halt, Sheriff Snow moved closer as he prepared to apprehend the wanted man. As he did so Clem raised a double-barreled shotgun that had been concealed at his side and leveled it at Sheriff Snow. Pulling his own sidearm, the sheriff drew a bead on Clem, and the two men found themselves engaged in a dangerous game of chicken. It would be Clem who first conceded, and slowly he lowered the shotgun until it was near his hip. Satisfied that he'd asserted his authority Sheriff Snow moved forward in order to complete the arrest. As he did so Clem seized the opportunity "to do for" an officer that he had lamented missing previously and fired from his hip. With the shot striking the ground well short of his intended target, a number of the pellets fired from Clem's gun ricocheted off of the ground and struck the sheriff's ankle, with a few more entering the pinky finger of his hand. Crying out that he'd been shot, Sheriff Snow would not be obstructed in the pursuit of his target. Surprisingly, the wounded sheriff was able to not only pursue Clem, but he also caught up to the much younger man as he attempted to escape. Declaring for the first, but not the last, time that he wished he had killed Sheriff Snow, Clem was apprehended and quickly given ten years in prison for attempted murder.

Serving eight of his ten-year sentence Clem was released in 1905 and again returned to Kalamazoo. Over the course of the next year he and his brother Vern would be arrested multiple times, with Clem routinely repeating his mantra that he wished he'd had a weapon to kill the officers who arrested him. Although the criminal undertakings of Clem and his brother were well known to authorities no officer was able to obtain evidence that would see the Bloods convicted. With Clem free to prowl the streets of Kalamazoo he soon initiated his most bizarre criminal endeavor to date. This particular scheme involved the attempted blackmail of his brother-in-law, Herbert Congdon (the same Herbert Congdon William Downey had apprehended back in 1887). In December of 1906, making no attempt to disguise the source, Clem sent Herbert a black-hand letter. Within was the demand that Herbert leave $100 in Clem's room, and if he did not Clem would use the dynamite he claimed to possess in a dastardly fashion. Herbert immediately reported the threat to authorities, and over the next few days Clem darted around the city as officers hunted for him. While he hid, he made numerous taunting phone calls to both Herbert and the authorities.

Although he had managed to frustrate officers to no end, and had successfully avoided apprehension, Clem soon realized that his ability to operate in Kalamazoo unimpeded had been significantly diminished. Fleeing, the wanted man was not heard from again in Kalamazoo until 1909 when a bearded Clem Blood returned to the city. While he may have thought that in his absence the authorities would have forgotten his crimes, or the addition of some facial hair would provide him with an ample disguise, he was predictably identified and apprehended. Although there was no doubt that he had sent the threatening letter in 1906, officers were still unable to secure evidence that would see Clem convicted. Unable to send him to prison where he belonged, and fed up with having an individual of his character in Kalamazoo, Sheriff Campbell gave Clem explicit instructions to leave Kalamazoo and never come back. With little recourse but to comply, Clem again left the city.

Drifting only a short distance Clem soon formed a small

gang in Grand Rapids, MI. In his role as Fagin to the impressionable boys who he surrounded himself with Clem would often entertain with tales of the glories of robbery and burglary. One seemingly innocuous young man who listened attentively to these stories was Arthur Shellhorn. Clem soon singled out Shellhorn as a morally malleable individual and endeavored to persuade him to join him in a job. Shellhorn eventually agreed, and as they contemplated their options it was Shellhorn who suggested they rob a local grocer by the name of Marinus Landman. Satisfied, Clem initiated a three-day period of reconnaissance during which it was observed that Mr. Landman's evening routine took him from his market to a secluded spot near a bridge that spanned the train tracks. That isolated location, Clem decided, would provide the pair with all of the privacy they required to complete their evil deed. With the planning done the pair took up a position near the bridge, ready to spring their trap. Near 10 p.m., as they knew he would, the unsuspecting Mr. Landman approached. As the grocer passed by Clem shouted, "Hit him, damn you, hit him!" and Shellhorn compliantly swung at the startled man's head with a sock that contained a number of jagged rocks. As Mr. Landman stumbled from the initial jolt Shellhorn had given him, Clem knocked the man down and struck him another strong blow to the head. Clem then dragged Mr. Landman under the bridge where he proceeded to beat him severely. The body of the dead or dying Mr. Landman was then thrust down the 30-foot embankment at the side of the railroad tracks.

Although a man named William Watts had seen two men running from the scene shortly before he discovered Mr. Landman's body, he was not able to identify the murderers due to the time of night. Clem and his accomplice very easily may have gotten away with the crime if it wasn't for one of the young men in Clem's gang. This conscionable youth soon reported his knowledge of the event to the police, and Clem was promptly apprehended. When asked why he had killed Mr. Landman, Clem responded that the grocer had looked up and recognized his face; then he chillingly remarked, "Dead men tell no tales." Within just one day of his arrest for Mr. Landman's murder Clem was on his way to Marquette Prison for the remainder of his natural life. While many were happy to have the 36-year-old habitual criminal removed from the community, others bemoaned the fact that he had not been separated from society earlier, with many suspecting that the aptly named Blood had left a long list of victims over the years for which he would never be held to account.

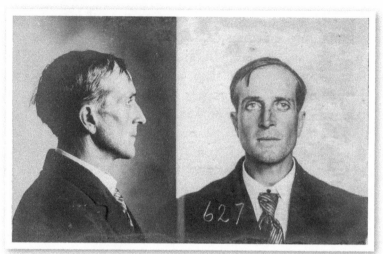
Mugshot of Clem Blood taken in 1910.
From the Collections of the Grand Rapids Museum.

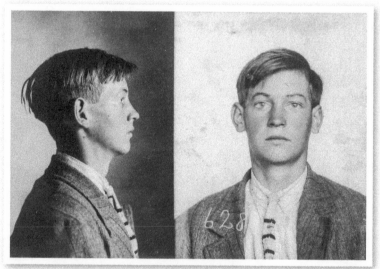
Mugshot of Arthur Shellhorn taken in 1910.
From the Collections of the Grand Rapids Museum

The widow Schilling, her daughters, and son-in-law Charles Drummond
picnic in what is now Milham Park c1894.
From the collection of the Kalamazoo Public Library

CHAPTER 16:
The Murderer Caught
The Weekly Expositor, February 09, 1894

FOLLOWING BILL WHITE's dismissal as a credible suspect the wind seemed to spill from the sails of the Schilling murder investigation. A man named Otto Piotter was detained in early April due to the accounts of several witnesses who had seen him enter the Schilling Market shortly after noon on the day of the murder. Although he had been seen entering the market via the front door, and there appears to be no other reason to suspect he had committed murder, officers claimed that he had given some contradictory statements when questioned, and the aggrieved Piotter was held for nearly a week before being released. Officers had also continued in their efforts to locate the farmer who had entered the Schilling Market twice on the day of the murder and was likely the red-faced man seen by numerous women as he fled south down Portage St. Although Sheriff's Deputy Thomas Warren and Sheriff Vosburg would both eventually travel to Elkhart, Indiana to question a man matching the farmer's description, they were unable to secure evidence or even the slightest indication that the man had played a part in the murder. Sheriff Vosburg would later state that numerous suspicioned men were closely watched throughout the remainder of 1893, but little further substantive progress into securing evidence against anyone was made.

Looking east down Main towards Portage Street c1894. *Art Work of Kalamazoo Volume 8.*

With the investigation sputtering a petition was numerously signed in mid-April asking the trustees to increase the reward for information leading to the capture of Louis Schilling's murderer from $500 to $1000. It wasn't until June that the trustees decided to comply, and Sheriff Vosburg posted notices of the increased sum in the local papers. The now substantial incentive was widely considered too little too late, and optimism regarding the capture of Louis Schilling's murderer slowly waned, while other events began to push the Schilling murder into the background of local consciousness. On May 1st thousands of people, out of an eventual twenty-seven million, flocked to the opening of the Chicago Worlds Fair. As accounts of the grandiose exhibitions filled the summer pages of local papers, Kalamazoo hosted its own celebration on the 4th of July, drawing twenty-five thousand attendants to the fairgrounds in celebration of the opening of Kalamazoo's new electric railway system. And while instances of puzzling criminal behavior still took place, such as Herbert Tyson's slaughterhouse mysteriously burning to the ground in August and Bill White being stabbed in the back by an unknown assailant on North Burdick St. a few weeks later, the occurrence of serious crimes had diminished when compared to the previous summer. For a time it appeared that the Schilling murder would not only go unsolved but would also be quickly forgotten; that was until January 18, 1894 when Sheriff Vosburg received the following letter from the Berrien County sheriff's office.

"DEAR SIR: -Enclosed find letter which is a mystery to me. Perhaps you may be able to connect it with something in the case. This letter was handed to a neighbor to be given to me. I have investigated the matter and I know the man. Am sure he wrote and sent the letter himself. He is a stranger to me, but he has been working in a restaurant in Kalamazoo and came from there here. I don't know just when. Some time last summer I think. Please send me the letter back if you have no use for it, or keep it so if I should want it I can get it. If you should want him wire me at Bridgman.

Yours, etc.

W. Teft Deputy Sheriff.

P.S. – Alguire is a cook and worked in a restaurant as cook. I understand you can locate him there and when he left."

The letter referenced by Deputy Sheriff Teft was enclosed and read as follows.

"Mr. Sheriff: -I have found man I have followed so long. Now you arrest him for the murder of Schilling of Kalamazoo last summer. You and I will have the reward offered***Waste no time. I will be on hand in due time. You know him."

Rightfully elated to finally be on the cusp of a breakthrough Sheriff Vosburg responded immediately requesting more information regarding the man Alguire who claimed to be in possession of such valuable information. The Berrien County sheriff's office had accurately anticipated that Sheriff Vosburg would be receptive and had already made contact with Alguire.

Originally from Royalton, MI near St. Joseph, little is known about William Alguire before he interjected himself into the Schilling murder case. During questioning by the Berrien County sheriff's department the 26-year-old Alguire told officers that he had arrived in Kalamazoo in January of

1893. Shortly thereafter he had secured a position for himself as a cook in the restaurant of Horace Mansfield on the corner of Water and N. Burdick Streets. In his position as cook Alguire had a divorcee who worked under him by the name of Anna Wood. Anna lived in a room over the Mansfield Restaurant, and it was here that Alguire claimed to have first heard the gestating schemes that would eventually lead to Louis Schilling's murder. As he explained to officers, sometime in early to mid-March, Alguire had ascended to Anna Wood's room and there overheard her and an unidentified man concocting a strategy to acquire Louis Schilling's money. As he eavesdropped he ascertained that Anna's role was that of a lookout, and she was to leave her room in the forenoon each day to observe Louis Schilling's banking activities. Anna was then to report back to the heretofore unnamed man who was secreted away in her room and who would later emerge to carry out the robbery. During the afternoon of March 21ˢᵗ, shortly after the murder had been committed, Alguire claimed that he had again visited Anna's room to find the unnamed man sitting on her bed in his stocking feet with his coat off, the implication being that his shoes and jacket were removed as they were covered in blood. Alguire claimed that he had then watched as Anna disposed of the murder weapon.

Over the ensuing days officers in Berrien County requested that Alguire recount this story to them multiple times. Although he would add a detail here or there his story did not waver significantly from the one he'd originally told. Writing down the key facts of his testimony officers sent the details to Sheriff Vosburg who then compared them to the known facts of the Schilling case. Finding Alguire's account a seemingly perfect match Sheriff Vosburg became increasingly confident of Alguire's legitimacy. Shortly thereafter he traveled to Berrien

County in order to collect the witness who seemed all too willing to accompany the sheriff.

Alguire's first stop when brought to Kalamazoo was the office of Prosecuting Attorney Frost where he was sworn in. He was then instructed to re-tell his tale full of nefarious plans, secret dealings in the room of Anna Wood, and the "mystery man" who had not yet been named. Throughout the ensuing interviews officials attempted to pry the name of this man from Alguire's lips, but for some reason unknown to them Alguire remained vague. When pressed on the issue, Alguire realized that the officers would not relent until he elaborated, and he soon told them that the mystery man was between 30 and 35, not very tall, weighed between 175 and 190 pounds, wore a brown suit, and had a small mustache. Although Alguire had been noticeably reticent in his description of the alleged murderer, Anna Wood and Herbert Mansfield were both arrested the following day.

It is at this point in the William Alguire saga that the case Sheriff Vosburg was hoping to build began to crumble. Shortly after Alguire arrived in Kalamazoo, it was discovered that he was an opium eater and laudanum addict. Although he was said to appear bright and responsive in conversation, his addiction did little to bolster his credibility. It was also soon discovered that he had made numerous untruthful statements to the officers that had taken his statements, including the fact that he had rather inexplicably lied about his own age. He had also implied that the killer was "not very tall," but the man officers had arrested, Herbert Mansfield, was 6'2". He in no way fit the description of the man that Alguire described and at his height was very unlikely to be the man who left size eight or nine footprints in the alley behind the market. It was also pointed out that if Alguire, Wood, and Mansfield were all in Anna's room shortly after the murder it would have been fairly noticeable given the fact that those three individuals made up the near entirety of the Mansfield Restaurant staff. Alguire would later go on to claim that the murderer was a third unnamed party, but his credibility was all but depleted when it was learned that he had married Anna Wood two months after the murder had occurred, with the two then divorcing shortly thereafter. With his story exploded William Alguire soon found himself housed in jail as the people he had implicated were set free.

Having come to the realization that Alguire was likely a liar and nothing more Sheriff Vosburg released him a few weeks later. As he would go on to do numerous times William Alguire again attempted to embroil himself in the Schilling case in May of 1894 when he changed his story and admitted to holding down Louis Schilling as his throat was cut. He would later recant this confession and proved perfectly willing to tell any tale he thought may be believed. As eager as local officers had initially been to bring Alguire to Kalamazoo to hear his testimony, by 1895 they couldn't wait to be rid of the man. In the year since he had confessed to taking part in the Schilling murder Alguire had made a game of writing letters to officers within which he would admit to being guilty of this or that offense. He would then dodge around and attempt to stay outside the reach of the law. In August of 1895, Sheriff Vosburg received one such letter, which read:

"If you want the man that got that 22 dollars and other stuff in the drug store block just look for me for I got that and if you do not believe it just ask that woman in that little brick house back of the store where they have rooms to rent and se(sic) if I did not rom(sic) at that time so I am here just now and hope you want me so I will never get no worse than I am and I forged that note on the City Creamery to so today I wrote here but no longer and yours as ever

WM. Alguire"

In contrast to what his many confessions may lead one to believe, the only crime William Alguire is known to have ever actually committed (other than perjury) was the forgery to the tune of $1.50 at the City Creamery he mentioned in the above letter. To the pleasure of local officers Alguire finally did move away and was not heard of again in Kalamazoo for nearly eight years when word of his death was received from Grand Rapids. It transpired that one evening in June of 1903, Alguire sat down to write a note to his wife. Perhaps with more honesty than in any other letter he had previously written he detailed his inability to break himself of his drug habit. He then ingested large amounts of morphine and alcohol and laid down on the couch in his family home on South Division St. Although his wife had found him shortly thereafter, and summoned a physician, William Alguire was pronounced dead at roughly 5 a.m. the next morning.

Mugshot of Milo Keep taken in 1905.
Courtesy of The Zhang Collections Center- Western Michigan University

CHAPTER 17:
Milo Keep the Criminal

"If his words be false, he is the most monumental liar that ever sat behind the bars of a prison. If his story be true, Milo Keep is the most wronged man in Kalamazoo today. If he be acquitted – he will have to move away and wander about the face of the earth, a miserable outcast until the grim reaper overtakes him"

WHATEVER POTENTIAL MILO Keep may have possessed as a youth, his familial circumstances did little to help him fulfill it. The paterfamilias of the Keep household was the one-eyed Darius Keep who lived off of a series of menial jobs and a small veteran's pension (Darius did not lose his eye in combat but had it removed in 1860 due to an infection he'd contracted while in jail for stealing a cow). When Milo was born in 1877, his older brother William was already a young man of nearly fifteen. A passing train had killed Milo's older sister Olive in 1869 well before he was born, and Milo's mother Emma had separated from his father when Milo was still young, leaving him solely under the questionable influence of his father and teenage brother. Milo was arrested for the first time at just nine years of age when he and some other boys broke into the home of local physician Charles Long on East Kalamazoo Ave. Although Judge Peck suspected the crime to have been the result of the negative influence of his peers, future events suggest that Milo's activities were more likely the outcome of what he had been taught at home. Before he'd reached his twenties he had spent nearly three years behind bars, and although his father and brother had had few run-ins with the law during Milo's adolescence, in 1897 the citizens of Kalamazoo would finally find out exactly what the entire Keep family had been up to.

It is safe to assume that William Duggan seldom hosted visitors. His two-story hovel south of Butterfield Lake near Richland had a smell that could turn the stomach of a tannery dog. Bits of fried salt pork were left about the house on unwashed plates, and it was said that the flies that once shared his meals soon found the stench too overpowering to remain and moved out. While his living conditions may have given the impression that he was destitute, the venerable Mr. Duggan was still a working farmer who often had money in his pockets. Such was the case in early August 1897 when he sold a cow and some wool. After seeing to his affairs at the Galesburg bank, Mr. Duggan returned home with $35 in his pocketbook. Just a few days later, on August 13th, Mr. Duggan finished pumping water for his cows shortly past noon and ambled back to his house via the side kitchen door. As he crossed the threshold two previously concealed men rushed up behind him. Brutally striking Mr. Duggan over the head the men then pursued him into the kitchen as the aging but nevertheless physically capable farmer attempted to defend himself. At one point raising his left arm to protect his head, the ensuing blow from one of the attackers snapped two bones of Mr. Duggan's forearm in half. Bleeding profusely from nearly a dozen head wounds and with one arm lame, Mr. Duggan soon appeared near death. With their victim satisfactorily incapacitated the two assailants then removed Mr. Duggan's pocket book (overlooking some change in his pocket) and grabbed a handful of other items before fleeing north through a cornfield. Although the attackers may have thought the elderly man dead, Mr. Duggan was not yet lifeless. Composing himself, the battered farmer stumbled a quarter of a mile to the farm of H. O. Bowker where word of the attack was sent to Sheriff Snow in Kalamazoo. When officers responded to Mr. Duggan's home, they found the normally unkempt living quarters to be in complete disarray. Signs of the struggle were readily evident, as were the tracks of the fleeing perpetrators. Two men wearing smallish shoes—one pointed, one square toed—had clearly set off on a lively run away from the Duggan residence. As officers followed the tracks they made the productive discovery of a small homemade cudgel that appeared to have been used in the attack. Unfortunately, as they trailed onward the tracks led officers to a point near a stream where they were lost. Over the following months all subsequent efforts to ascertain the identities of the attackers proved unproductive.

There is a very real likelihood that the men who attacked Mr. Duggan would have gone unidentified if it were not for the efforts of a number of his frustrated neighbors who for months had also experienced the loss of their own personal property. Although none of them had been physically attacked as Mr. Duggan had, the constant disappearance of valued items had exceeded many of the local citizens' capacity for patience. In October, two months after the attack on Mr. Duggan, Albert Chase and his wife began the nocturnal practice of keeping watch over their property in shifts. After six nights of vigilance the Chases observed the midnight raid of two nefarious looking men. The Chases quickly alerted their neighbors, Messrs. Stratton and Brazee, who volunteered to follow the two suspected lawbreakers. For miles the amateur sleuths shadowed the shady characters until one of the men led them all the way to downtown Kalamazoo and the residence of William Keep.

The entire affair was then reported to Sheriff Snow, whose initial reaction erred towards indifference. Unsatisfied, the Chases and their neighbors demanded a search of Darius Keep's house near Richland. Relenting, Sheriff Snow obtained a warrant and along with a number of officers headed to Richland to inspect the Keep property.

What officers found when they arrived was a veritable thieves' den of ill-gotten gains. Items incriminating the Keeps in acts of larceny were everywhere, but it wasn't just evidence of theft that officers located. Near the front door, hanging on the wall, was a whip that had curiously had its handle removed. Continuing their exploration officers soon discovered that one of Darius's toolboxes contained some very unique pieces of fox squirrel leather. When the cudgel found near the William Duggan assault was brought to the Keep home and dismantled, the modified whip and squirrel leather found during the search fit together perfectly with the homemade weapon. Darius Keep, who had initially been boisterous and indignant when the search had begun, was presented with this discovery and became sullen. Darius and Milo were both brought to the jail and charged with the easily provable crime of steeling sheep. As William Keep did not live with Darius and Milo he temporarily avoided apprehension. His freedom would be short lived, however, as Sheriff Snow was diligently working to build a case for the much more serious charge of attempted murder. In order to secure the confession that would allow him to arrest William, Sheriff Snow decided to target the youngest and most impressionable of the Keep gang. When the mountain of evidence against him was presented, Milo very quickly confessed. He then explained to the sheriff that his father had planned the crime and that he and another man had carried it out. Although Milo would not initially name his cohort, Sheriff Snow had little doubt that the other man was his older brother, and William was also arrested. With all three Keeps now incarcerated in the county jail pending trial Milo was housed in an upstairs cell away from his father and brother so that they could not influence his planned testimony. While the effort to preserve the integrity of Milo's testimony was certainly prudent, perhaps more care should have been taken to ensure that he was still incarcerated long enough to testify.

One evening, shortly after his arrest, Milo requested a razor with which to shave. He then tore his bed sheets into strips and fashioned for himself a makeshift rope. As the jail staff busied themselves in other areas he climbed his cell door to the rods above. Using the razor he then cut out two pieces of board and climbed out onto the roof. After replacing the slate behind him he scoured the rooftop until he found a suitable spot to secure his makeshift rope and began his decent. Unfortunately Milo had misjudged the strength of his crude rope, and with his full weight born by the sheets they ripped. Milo fell what was not an insignificant distance to the ground below before hobbling away. When it was later discovered that he had escaped, a resulting search of the grounds uncovered a remaining impression in the ground at the point where he had impact-fully landed.

With Milo in the wind the sheriff's office quickly posted notice of a $100 reward for his return. They then enlisted the help of a local tracker, whose team of bloodhounds could soon be heard excitedly barking all over the city. Although a hard rain had somewhat concealed his trail, after two days of painfully creeping about Milo began to grow increasingly fearful of the encroaching dogs. Afraid, and in no physical condition to run, he decided to give himself up. Waiting until dark Milo emerged from his hiding place within the straw of a local barn and shuffled slowly back to the jail. When he arrived around 11 p.m., he snuck back inside. When Undersheriff Eberstein arrived early the next morning to continue his search for Milo, he was surprised to find his quarry curled up in a chair in the sheriff's office.

During the trial that followed Milo took the stand as he had promised to do and confessed to his involvement in the attack on Mr. Duggan. For his cooperation Milo was given some consideration and received a sentence of seven years in Jackson State Prison. The trials of Darius and William soon followed with similarly favorable results for the prosecution. After just one hour of deliberation the jury found Darius Keep guilty. Due to his advanced age (he claimed to be 80 but was in fact 73) the jury asked for leniency, and Darius was given a sentence of three years. A month later, William was given the lengthiest sentence of the bunch when he was sentenced to Jackson for nine years. Following his conviction the facade of the previously stoic William Keep cracked for the first time, and on the way out of court he asked Undersheriff Eberstein to take him and hang him to a lamppost. With all three Keeps behind bars many in Kalamazoo were very satisfied to have what was considered to be one of the most prolific criminal gangs in the area out of commission. An estate sale at Darius's property was later organized and was comically interrupted by repeated cries of, "Wait, don't sell that, it belongs to me!"

Looking south from the intersection of Main and Portage Streets in the early twentieth century. The space formerly occupied by the Schilling Market is just visible on the right side of the image between the two three-story buildings.

From the collection of the Kalamazoo Valley Museum

CHAPTER 18:
"Tom Warren Is a Great Big Shitepoke"
A.A. Hazard August 1887

I N JANUARY OF 1899, the *Kalamazoo Gazette* ran their last article of the 19th century devoted solely to the Schilling case. The purpose of the belated and somewhat suppositious article was the recent boisterous declarations of former police officer and sometime private detective Thomas Warren. As he would up until his dying day in 1906, Warren not only claimed to know who the perpetrators of the Schilling murder were but stated that he could put his hands on the slayer anytime he wanted. Unfortunately, the reputation of Thomas Warren is as complicated as the mystery surrounding the murder itself, leaving his audience to entertain his theories or totally disregard them depending how amenable they are to accept his competence.

On October 10, 1884, a special council meeting was held wherein the predominant subject of conversation was the assault of one police officer at the hands of another. Addressing the mayor and members of the council, the city's first marshal, Stephen H. Wattles, did allege that Special Policeman Thomas Warren had thrown Policeman Boekeloo to the ground, breaking his leg below the knee. Marshal Wattles, who had appointed Warren to his position as policeman, then followed this allegation with another aimed at Boekeloo, who he alleged had been drunk on the job, neglected his duties, and had a general quarrelsome attitude with his fellow officers. When the examination into Warren's actions took place a few weeks later, he was found guilty of the assault, and the committee called for his immediate removal from the newly formed city police force. Officer Boekeloo, who was still recovering from his injuries, was not called to appear until one month after Warren's dismissal. When the date finally did arrive, numerous witnesses would testify that not only was Officer Boekeloo not a drunk, but they couldn't seem to find a single person who could say they had ever seen the man intoxicated. William Downey was even roped into the authentication of Officer Boekeloo's innocence, as the over-zealous Warren had apparently tried to enlist passersby to help him arrest William on the same night that he had broken Boekeloo's leg. In the end Officer Boekeloo was cleared of any wrongdoing, and Warren was made to look quite foolish. But as it has many times before, nepotism would save a floundering career, and Warren's dismissal from the police force would prove to be only temporary.

During the ongoing career of Thomas Warren there were undoubtedly instances of legitimate police work, but these were regularly overshadowed by his well-publicized missteps. In support I present to you the following quote from 1887.

"In the main, the Kalamazoo police force is composed of faithful and efficient officers, but contains a few who are notoriously incompetent and utterly unfit for the positions they hold. Prominent among the latter is Thomas Warren, who during the brief period he has been upon the force has not only caused himself to be the laughing stock of all acquainted with his amateur detective methods, but has also conducted himself in a manner that richly merits a coat of tar and feathers as punishment."

Conspicuous among the complaints levied against Warren around the time of this quote were the allegations that he had nearly started a riot on the corner of Main and Burdick Streets. Numerous witnesses would later testify that around 10 p.m. on August 20, 1887 policeman Warren seized on an opportunity to exploit his position and bully some local youths who were out on the town. As he blustered in the faces of the revelers, a crowd of nearly a hundred people gathered with most of them jeering at the actions of the officer. Defiant, Warren picked out an older man of slight proportions from the crowd and proceeded to handle him quite roughly. The crowd responded by shouting for Warren to release the man, which he quickly did. With the mob around him growing in size and anger, Warren was soon on the verge of losing control. Fortunately for him Officer Verberg soon discovered the commotion and came to Warren's aid. As the two officers pranced up and down defiantly rebuking the mob, someone shoved John "Blondy" Bright into the side of Warren. Grasping the opportunity to save face and extricate themselves from the situation, the two officers led Blondy away as the crowd that had reached nearly three hundred individuals howled behind them. Although Blondy was quickly released from jail, he had been struck six times with a club and had lost $6 in the process of being arrested. A charge of assault and battery was quickly brought against Warren, although significant repercussions were not forthcoming. Policeman Warren retained his job, but public sentiment was growing increasingly negative towards him. The community's opinion of the man was only diminished by the pervasive rumors that the rather infamous lawman had been spending a large percentage of his days peeking in windows and watching women at unwanted times. With allegations of police brutality, peeping, and general boorish behavior Warren become a liability. In order to mitigate his continued annoyances the city managers allowed him to retire prematurely with a disability pension.

Thomas Warren engaged in private business pursuits until 1893 when the election of his political ally William Vosburg would lead to the continuation of his law enforcement career and his involvement in the Schilling murder case. Hired as a deputy in mid-March, Warren made his first arrest in his new position within the sheriff's department just a few days before Louis Schilling was murdered. Although he would go on to take part in the investigation, Warren would later claim that egregious mistakes had been made (by others) in the execution of securing evidence. After years of conducting his own private inquiry into the murder, which some claimed had begun around the time that the considerable reward had been offered, Warren was said to have in his possession a substantial bundle of pertinent documents. The first account of the methods used by Warren to secure the evidence supposedly found in his files comes from January 1896 when Kalamazoo City Supervisors were presented with a claim requesting the refund of a fine of $21 given to James Campbell. It seems that Warren had enlisted Campbell as some kind of undercover snoop. Campbell's instructions, per Warren, were to inundate individuals suspected of the Schilling murder with alcohol and, once they were drunk, elicit a confession. Campbell did not prove to be skilled in this position and got so drunk that he himself was arrested. Campbell was then given the sizable fine of $21, which Warren would argue should be waved due to the earnest motivations that led Campbell to drink. The only clue as to whom Warren had instructed Campbell to target with this ploy is the man arrested for drunkenness with Campbell, John Collins. Collins had been arrested in Kalamazoo in August '92 for robbery, but there is no other indication that he was involved or even suspected by anyone else as the murderer. It is safe to say that Warren was never able to trick Collins or any other drunk into confessing, but this failed tactic did not stop him from continuing to work the case. Warren unrelentingly added to his findings until 1899 when he delivered his documents to Prosecuting Attorney Master. Warren would later state that the prosecutor agreed with him that mistakes had originally been made in the way the investigation had been handled; but nevertheless the prosecutor was unwilling or unable to indict those implicated by Warren's work. Unfortunately, no known record exists of the party or parties whom Warren suspected in 1899, but he did leave a few clues that may allow someone willing to entertain a certain leap of presumption to deduce his suspicions.

At the time that Warren submitted his findings to the prosecutor in January 1899, he stated that the parties who killed Louis Schilling were having a hard time keeping one of their associates quiet. He claimed that this potential loose wheel was being plied with a pint of whiskey daily in order to satisfy his cravings and keep him silent. While Warren did not publically identify this whiskey wreck, a familiar name had recently been added to the logbook at the county jail on a charge of drunkenness, George Tyson. George was certainly passible as a whiskey wreck. There were also undoubtedly those in Kalamazoo who had noticed that the alibi George had provided Bill White had contradicted the testimony of at least four others. If Warren had his suspicions regarding George's involvement in the Schilling murder he was certainly not the only one.

Just two months after making the aforementioned remarks

in 1899, Warren would again find himself embroiled in a curious situation involving another individual connected to the Brooks' slaughterhouse. The details vague, the general gist of the situation seems to have been the instigation of a donny-brook between twenty to thirty men attending a local political event. Interestingly, upon the outbreak of said donny-brook Warren was said to have rushed into the hostile ring. Whether his purpose in doing so was to engage in fisticuffs or break up the fight is not known. What is known is that one of the initial combatants, and bloodied loser during the violence, was James Colligan. Astute readers will recognize the familiar name as it was James's brother "Tame" Colligan who was brought in under suspicion for the Schilling murder and later released. What Warren knew that you might not is that James Colligan was George Tyson's longtime partner in the meat business.

While this information is far from definitive, it does seem to suggest that in 1899, when he submitted his findings to the prosecutor, Warren was paying particular attention to individuals associated with the Brooks' slaughterhouse. It also seems that neither the prosecutor nor any other in Kalamazoo treated his findings with the amount of significance he felt they deserved. With his suspects unprosecuted, his notes lost, and his reputation questionable the lawman that pursued the murderer for more years than any other leaves us little meaningful insight into who killed Louis Schilling.

Local Election

Cast a Vote for Good Government Tomorrow

The candidates for constables, William S. Downey, Andrew Stewart, John Kretzenger, John DeSmit, Jr. They are reliable, hard workers, and all are men of good judgment.

April 01, 1900

Noted Travelers Arrive in Town

A Gang of "vags" ran into an exceedingly warm reception when the "Cannon Ball" freight arrived in this city this morning at 12:20. Patrolman Stearns, Tatroe, Todd, and Dingman and Assistant Chief William Downey were on hand and captured four of the gang. Two of the fellos jumped from the train before it stopped and escaped. Another started up Church St and Assistant Chief Downey ordered him to stop, but he refused and four bullets were sent after him, but he still kept going. They were a tough looking gang and had evidently been in some crooked work somewhere and were anxious to get away.

July 28, 1900

Think They Are Burglars:
Officers Arrest Two Suspicious Characters

The officers made a catch of two men Monday afternoon and evening whom Assistant Chief of Police Downey believes are the men who committed the recent house burglaries in this city. The men gave their names as Perry Unrich and George Kelley. They are well dressed and the officers believe them to be a pair of first class crooks. Unrich was arrested Monday evening at the Wilbur home west of the city by Assistant Chief of Police Downey and Deputy Sheriff Sanford. Kelley was arrested Monday evening by Assistant Chief of Police Downey and Detective Harper.
August 28, 1900

Cut Both Tires

Somebody Disabled Assistant Chief of Police Downey's Wheels.
July 11, 1901

Police Got A Nine Spot

Nine people, including the proprietor, were arrested at Butine's stall saloon in east Main St. Tuesday night about 10:30 o'clock by Assistant Chief of Police Downey and Patrolman Frentheway
April 16, 1902

Melissa Harrison, ex-wife of Milo Keep.
Kalamazoo Gazette, May 03, 1905

CHAPTER 19:
Milo Keep the Murderer

"I believe that Milo Sexton, Milo Keep as he is known to some, is the man who murdered my nephew, Bert Miller, Monday night in my rooming house at 121 West Water St. I hope that Milo will be convicted and sent up for life. I loved him once, but hate him now. I will never get married again" Melissa Harrison May 2, 1905

ALTHOUGH MILO'S RECORD while in prison was not unblemished (he was recommended for transfer to the State House of Correction in Marquette in 1902 due to his incorrigible behavior) he was able to secure an early release in 1904. The relatively short sentences of not only Milo but also his brother and father were particularly generous when you consider that William Duggan never recovered from the beating the Keeps had given him and had died shortly thereafter in 1900. Irrespective of their victim's fate, all three of the Keeps were prematurely free to return to Kalamazoo, and it wouldn't be long before Milo would once again be front-page news.

In August of 1904, Milo made the acquaintance of local construction worker W. O. Mclaughlin who offered him a position assisting with his cement business. This arrangement lasted less than four months, and in November the partnership was ended. W.O. would later claim that he'd caught Milo stealing from him, and while this is certainly possible, it also seems that jealousy over a woman played a role in the abbreviated business relationship. Up until a few months before he'd met Milo, W.O. had been married to Melissa Harrison. Melissa was a woman with dark snappy eyes, hair like a raven's wing, and a commanding presence. She was also known to run a boarding house where she would rent rooms by the night or the hour to any man and woman who told her they were married. Melissa would later become infamous in Kalamazoo when the papers would report on the occurrence of her eighth marriage. In 1904, however, W.O. was just her third husband, and Milo would soon become the fourth. Later stating that his relationship with Melissa had begun in the backrooms of local saloons where she'd relentlessly pursued him, Milo claimed that his future wife had eventually worn him down with wedding proposals until he acquiesced. The two were married on December 22, 1904 with Milo choosing to use the surname of Sexton and listing both of his parents as "unknown" on their marriage license in an apparent attempt to hide his criminal past from his new wife.

Unsurprisingly, the marriage of Mr. and Mrs. Milo Sexton was short-lived, with the "honeymoon" barely lasting four months. On April 26, 1905, Melissa filed for divorce, and Milo was forced to move out of the rooms Melissa rented out over Van Peenen's Saloon on Water St. Shortly thereafter, Melissa's twenty-nine-year-old nephew Bert Miller left his wife in Battle Creek and moved into one of his aunt's rooms. Bert's family would later claim that he'd moved to Kalamazoo in order to secure steady work and intended to send for his wife when he did so. Others theorized that Bert had moved in with Melissa in order to protect her from Milo. There were even implications that Bert and his aunt Melissa were engaged in an inappropriate physical relationship. Milo would later downplay the more salacious of these notions and claimed that he and Bert had always been on the best of terms. All of these theories and more would soon be scrutinized when on the morning of May 2nd, 1905, Melissa made her way to Bert's room to wake him for breakfast only to find her nephew murdered in his bed.

Image of the Bert Miller murder scene
taken exclusively for the Kalamazoo Gazette. May 03, 1905

When officers responded to the scene around 8 a.m., they found the body of Bert Miller lying on its side as if he were still asleep. Blood seeped from a wound just behind the left ear where a single devastating blow had crushed Bert's skull. The search of the crime scene that followed was a short one, as the room Bert occupied was little more than a closet with a low ceiling, barely large enough for the bed, washstand, and single chair contained within. The only light into the room came from a small window devoid of glass that opened into the hall rather than the outdoors. It was in the deep dust that had collected on the sill of this "window" that officers discovered a handprint. It was thought that the murderer had leaned on the sill in order to peek out into the hall before escaping and that the print had notably been left by someone with a crooked pinky finger on their right hand. Conveniently officers also discovered a two-foot rasp under the washstand. Although no blood was found on the tool it was thought to be the murder weapon without a doubt. Further easing the difficulty of deciphering the nature of the case, Melissa provided officers with a detailed theory regarding who had perpetrated the attack. With the events surrounding the murder appearing obvious deputy Sheriff Bean rather casually arrested Milo as he was walking down Water St. around 9:00 that same morning.

From the moment he was arrested the deck seemed to be stacked against Milo. The first attorney he had secured died just days before the trial was to begin. Milo then had significant difficulty raising capital to hire a replacement. He would later state that he did not understand that legal representation would be provided him if he could not afford it, which had caused him to rather desperately write letters to individuals he thought may provide him support or whom he thought he could coax into a confession in his stead. Eventually Darius Keep would come to his son's aid, and finances were secured with which Milo was able to hire spirited attorney Claude Ketcham.

The trial that followed was one of the most sensational and convoluted Kalamazoo ever experienced. Since the day of the murder inquisitive locals voraciously read the details of the case in the local papers. When the trial finally began, scores of anxious spectators crowded into the courtroom hoping to hear salacious details and further theorize about the crime. Many society women packed lunches and arrived early to secure prime seats for themselves as officers chased packs of youths from the courtroom in order to maintain the decorum of the proceedings. As the spectacle got underway there was an air of presumed guilt that lingered over the whole affair, which was summed up by prosecuting attorney Jackson when he rather portentously explained to the jury:

"It has been thoroughly demonstrated that a crime has been committed. This man (Milo Keep) made statements as to his previous whereabouts on the night of the murder, which he afterwards admitted were false. It has been established that he knew of the existence of this rasp file with which the physician has stated the wound in Miller's head could have been made."

Nothing in the aforementioned statement is necessarily false: Bert Miller had most certainly had his head staved in, and Milo had initially told officers that he had stayed with his brother William on the night of the murder, which William did not corroborate. And when Milo was then confronted about this lie, he invented another in which he claimed to have stayed with a woman he would not name. Given his criminal history and his reticence to tell the truth Milo admittedly looked susceptible to the prosecution's case against him. But therein lies the crux of the matter; the above facts represent the near entirety of the prosecution's case. Given the situation it should come as no surprise that Milo's attorney would make a special plea for Judge Adams to charge the jury on matters of circumstantial evidence.

The primary piece of physical evidence presented at Milo's trial was the rasp found in Bert Miller's room. As previously alluded to, this item was never proven to be the murder weapon as no blood was found on the tool. However, Coroner Verhage would testify at trial that during the autopsy a three-inch section of Bert's skull fell out in a shape that was thought consistent with a heavy blow from the rasp. In response Milo's attorney questioned whether the square-edged implement could have created a wound that appeared rounded. The defense also called Dr. Shillito who testified that such a wound would have been difficult for a man of Milo's slight proportions to inflict. With their establishment of the rasp as the murder weapon tentative the prosecution then attempted to connect it to Milo. This bit of circumstantial assemblage was made courtesy of Milo's former employer, W.O. Mclaughlin, who had come forward shortly after the murder to say that the rasp looked like one he had previously owned. W.O. claimed that during their brief business relationship Milo had used a rasp that looked very much like the one found at the murder scene and that it had been left in one of the rooms over Van Peenen's saloon after W.O. had moved out following his divorce from Melissa. At trial Milo made no attempt to dispute these facts and stated that he had used a similar looking rasp both during and after his employment with W.O. However, he denied any recent possession of the rasp, and no further evidence linking him to it or confirming it as the murder weapon was provided.

There were a few other bits of physical evidence that had once seemed to implicate Milo, but during trial serious doubt was cast as to their legitimacy. First, there were the fingerprints left on the windowsill that seemed to match quite well with the bent pinky finger of Milo's right hand. During trial Sheriff Shean and Deputy Sheriff Bean would both testify that they put little weight in the prints as the apparent crooked fingerprint could just as easily have been the result of the way someone had rested their hand on the sill. What was initially thought to be the damning evidence against Milo had lost its validity. Similarly, a spot thought to be blood that was noticed on Milo's shirt when he was arrested lost its significance when Dr. Crane testified that after x-ray and microscope examination the stain was likely tobacco juice. Milo's possession of a skeleton key was also brought up at trial as it was suggested he had recently purchased the item to gain entry to Bert Miller's room. As with the other items brought forward to implicate him there was no definitive evidence presented to show that the murderer had gained entry using a similar commonly owned key or that the key Milo owned had been used in the crime in any way.

Like much of the physical evidence that was presented at trial the initial theory given to officers by Melissa on the morning of the murder was also soon exploded. It had been Melissa's initial suggestion that Milo had entered her establishment during the day and had remained hidden until everyone had turned in for the night around 10:30. She speculated that Milo had then emerged from his hiding place before sneaking into Bert Miller's room. This was provably false as numerous people would go on to testify that they had seen Milo on the night in question up to nearly 10:30. This included William Keep who stated that although Milo did not spend the night in his room, his brother and two other men had visited him after dark. Other equally speculative theories regarding when and how Milo may have gained entrance into the building were floated during the trial, including the idea that he had climbed a bit of fence-work up to the second story of the building and another that had him picking an exterior lock. None of which reached the level of convincing.

With the theories regarding how he had executed the crime dubious, Milo's previous inability to account for where he had slept on the night of the murder remained a problematic aspect of his defense, that was until he was able to present his lawyer with a stub from the New England Restaurant written out for one of the rooms there on the night of the murder. Whether he'd acquired it illegitimately after the fact or it had been in his possession the whole time, the stub poked a significant hole in the prosecution's case against him. In response to the appearance of the seemingly exculpatory evidence Deputy Sheriff Bean testified that Milo had been thoroughly searched when arrested, and he believed the stub would have been located had it been in one of his pockets at that time. Additionally, Albert Cavanaugh who worked at the New England Restaurant testified that no man had stayed in any of the rooms on the night in question. However, under cross-examination Albert changed his testimony slightly to say that he did not know if Milo had stayed in one of the rooms. Where and when he acquired the stub or if Milo stayed at the New England Restaurant the night Bert Miller was killed was never conclusively ascertained during trial.

In one of their last efforts to implicate Milo the prosecution argued that no one unfamiliar with the rooms over the Van Peenen saloon could have committed the murder as the maze of dark corridors would have made finding Bert Miller's room impossible without foreknowledge of the building. The jury was even brought to the site and given a tour in order to illustrate this theory. It was later pointed out by the defense that Milo was not the only person who knew the layout of the building. Other men had visited and even lived there.

Like Milo, W.O. was a jilted lover who had resided in one of the rooms over the Van Peenen saloon. He had also expressed resentment towards Milo and at one point admitted to attacking and knocking Milo down when he saw him walking down the street with Melissa. W.O. had also linked himself to the suspected murder weapon, and after a bit of detective work Defense Attorney Ketcham secured the testimony of two women who would raise suspicions that it was W.O. who had committed the murder. Mrs. Vogel and her daughter would both testify that early on the morning that Bert Miller was found dead W.O. had visited the restaurant they operated. While there W.O. reportedly spoke loudly of the murder before the details had been made public or the police had even completed their investigation. The two women claimed that W.O. had specifically accused Milo of attacking Bert Miller and had gone so far as to describe the presence of paint on Milo's shoes, which he ascribed to Milo climbing to the second story of the boarding house. Unsurprisingly W.O. would later deny these statements and testified during trial that he had not heard of the murder until around noon when he spoke of it with a coworker.

At the close of the prosecution's case Judge Adams did charge the jury regarding reasonable doubt and circumstantial evidence as Defense Attorney Ketcham had asked him to do. Given his understanding of the burden of proof, Ketcham must have felt optimistic as the jury began their deliberations. Not only had the prosecution brought forward a very weak case against his client, but also public sentiment towards Milo had curiously begun to shift. Regardless of his shortcomings, of which he had many, Milo had retained an air of quiet dignity throughout the trial. He dressed sharply, groomed himself genteelly, and wore a number of pieces of jewelry that gave him the appearance of being a man well above his actual station. As the trial closed frequent were the claims from observers that there was still good in Milo, with young girls and their older sisters said to have begun to lionize the defendant. But trials are not always won in the court of public opinion, and to Defense Attorney Ketcham's dismay the jury quickly returned a verdict of guilty. Remaining calm as he had throughout the entire trial, Milo turned to his attorney and plainly stated, "You put up a good fight. You did all you could. They's got the wrong man."

After his conviction many in Kalamazoo remained divided in their opinions as to Milo's guilt, with some of his supporters going so far as to take up a collection to facilitate an appeal. Although his attorney would quickly begin preparations to file a motion for a new trial, no post-conviction effort proved productive, and Milo was soon on his way to Jackson Prison for life.

Asst. Chief Downey Dangerously Ill

W.S. Downey is reported in a serious condition. He has been confined to his bed for some time, and congestion of the lungs and liver have developed. It is feared that it may be necessary to remove him to a hospital unless a change for the better takes place soon.
April 23, 1903

White Under Arrest

William White, who for some time has refused to take care of his wife and children, was arrested yesterday afternoon by Patrolman William Downey. White has for some time made himself a nuisance to the community. He now has several children at Lansing and the remainder, who are here in the city, he refuses to support.
February 06, 1904

Sergeant Downey Firmly Believes
The Right Man is Serving Sentence

Sergeant William Downey, of the police department has read with interest the efforts that are being made by the relatives of George Taylor, a life convict in the Jackson prison to secure his pardon. Sergeant Downey was instrumental in bringing about the conviction of Taylor and he is firmly convinced of the man's guilt and he will do what he can if called upon to lay the facts before the pardon board.

November 5, 1905

Violate Liquor Laws

Charging violation of the liquor laws, a warrant is out for the arrest of John McLaughlin, proprietor of the City hotel. Sergeant Downey raided the hotel bar room last Sunday and found, so it is stated, about 15 persons in the room, many of them drinking.

June 27, 1905

Chief Boyles and
Sergeant Downey are out

Asked for and received the resignations of Sergeant William Downey, and Patrolman Del Glover of the Police Department. Announced, all changes in police department would be effective

June 1, 1906

Looking east down Main towards Portage Street c1868.
From the collection of the Kalamazoo Valley Museum

CHAPTER 20:
Guilty Free Are Enormous
Kalamazoo Gazette, February 11, 1906

As THE AUGHTS progressed it seemed as if the Schilling murder was on the verge of transitioning from a contemporary case into a bit of misremembered historical trivia. Even when the event did warrant a quick reflective mention in the local papers in 1904, the article gave the name of the murder victim as "Andrew Schilling." Not to be outdone, an article from 1906 referred to the murdered man as "August Schilling," who was at that time Louis's still living son. This level of accuracy was in keeping with the rest of the piece, which also referred to the murder of Thomas McAvey in the late 1860s as an "ancient puzzle." The only problem being that the murdered man was Thomas McEvoy, not McAvey. And unlike the article suggested, the case did not go unsolved. In fact, the "murderer" had reported the incident almost immediately to a police officer. The particulars are as follows.

A minstrel from New Orleans named James McIvor and a number of individuals of similar occupation were drinking together one evening in 1869 following the cancellation of a dance they were to attend at the Park House. Eventually ending up at Eagle's Saloon the men continued to partake in social consumption until there was an argument regarding who would pay for the night's libations. After an insinuation was made that James McIvor should be the one to do so, he attempted to make his exit. Thomas McEvoy and a man named Daggett proceeded to chase McIvor as he left. With McEvoy gaining on him, and undoubtedly fearing for his safety, James McIvor pulled out a pocketknife. Shouting over his shoulder as he fled McIvor stated that if McEvoy attacked him "he would be cut." Paying no heed to this warning Thomas McEvoy rushed James McIvor and seized him while simultaneously demanding money. Spinning, McIvor stabbed McEvoy between the fifth and sixth ribs, the blow severing his intercostal artery and entering the left auricle of the heart. Still in fear, James McIvor raced on to the Kalamazoo House where he relayed the events to a police officer. McIvor then returned to the scene with the officer where they found Thomas McEvoy dead. With numerous witnesses to the incident the coroner's jury found McIvor to have acted in self-defense, and no charges were brought against him. A far cry from the great unsolved crime it was made out to be in 1906, but then again the author couldn't get the first name of the most well-known murder victim in Kalamazoo history correct while members of the dead man's family still lived within the city.

Place For Downey

William Downey, former member of the police department has secured a fine position as a dock officer to look after the property of the Stockbridge estate at Mackinac Island. He will leave this morning and be gone most of the summer. Mr. Downey retired as a member of the police department a few weeks ago and is an efficient officer.
July 06, 1906

William Downey to Open Private Detective Agency

William S. Downey, one of the best known officers of Kalamazoo county has opened an office in the Brown block, rooms 302 and 303, and will conduct a detective agency. There seems to be considerable opportunity for such an establishment in Kalamazoo as the police and sheriff forces have their hands full all the time. Downey has had an exceedingly large experience as a criminal officer and detective and is well adapted to the work he has taken up. Downey will give to private business the same energy and prompt attention as he did when a police officer.
November 08, 1906

William Downey, the politician.
William Downey, the shrewd detective.
William Downey, the attorney.

The latest is his new role, and to William's credit it is said that he made a remarkably good showing. Kate Regan, charged with drunkenness, second offense, was his client. Downey entered his appearance before his honor in the same way a real attorney does. He then cross-examined the people's witnesses and placed his own client on the stand. No attempt was made by Downey to deny the fact that his client was a drunk-that was not the point. He wanted to show the court that while the Regan woman was addicted to drink, in nine cases out of ten someone else gave the booze to her. No attempt was made at oratorical flights. William talked slowly and with earnestness. The judge said he recognized the truth of Downey's contention, but said about 60 days in the Detroit workhouse would suit in the case.

October 9, 1907

The Worlds Greatest Seeress,
Madame Gertrude.
Kalamazoo Saturday Telegraph,
December 12, 1908

Murder victim Horace "Hal" Davis.
Kalamazoo Evening Telegraph,
November 26, 1907

CHAPTER 21:
"Who Killed Hal Davis!?"

WHEN THE NEWS began to circulate that Madame Gertrude, "the world's greatest seeress," was to have an engagement at the Majestic Theatre, many in Kalamazoo anxiously prepared their questions. When the enigmatic woman finally appeared to a packed theatre on December 12th, 1908, the credulous crowd reveled in her seemingly omniscient powers. Questions regarding the faithfulness of a spouse or the sex of an anticipated child were fielded with aplomb, but as Madame Gertrude answered the predictable questions one man in the balcony stood and unpredictably shouted, "Who killed Hal Davis?" Pausing, Madame Gertrude seemed flummoxed for the first time that evening. After a moment of consideration she responded that such an important query deserved further thought and promised to answer during a future engagement. Two days later, in a once again packed theatre, Madame Gertrude appeared to a crowd that was eagerly anticipating the clues that the seeress had divined. Although her exact answer is now unknown, the clairvoyant insights of Madame Gertrude regarding the identity of Mr. Davis's murderer were met with disappointment and consternation. Some found her visions into the case so ludicrously implausible that they questioned whether she was a true seeress at all or was just "cute".

Not since 1893 did a murder have such a profound effect

on Kalamazoo as that of Horace "Hal" Davis. Like Louis Schilling, 53-year-old Hal Davis was an established and respected Kalamazoo businessman who was mysteriously killed during the execution of a burglary. It was even revealed after his death that the Davises' bulldog had been found dead in the yard of their home at 413 South Burdick St. of an apparent poisoning shortly before the murder, with many theorizing that, similar to the Schilling family dog, the faithful pet had been dispatched in preparation of a robbery. The murder of Mr. Davis also caused a long absent wave of fear to wash over the community, as demonstrated by some five hundred concerned citizens who purchased revolvers from local shopkeepers in the weeks following the Davis murder. For those old enough to remember the Schilling murder a sense of déjà vu crept into their minds, but for all of their similarities there was one major difference that separated the Davis murder from the Schilling case, and that was the presence of a witness to the heinous crime.

Early in the morning of November 26th, 1907 near 03:45, Mrs. Davis was awoken by a jingling noise she would later describe as sounding as if a cat had walked over her china cabinet. Opening her eyes and raising her head the faint glow of a flashlight near the foot of her bed illuminated the form of a strange masked man. "What do you want? Get out of here!" she called out to the darkness. In response the dark figure pushed a .38 revolver into Mrs. Davis's face and in a menacing voice barked, "Keep still or I will blow your brains out." The presence of the unfamiliar man's voice was enough to rouse Mr. Davis, and in a flash he leapt from the bed to confront the intruder. As the two men jostled in darkness, Mrs. Davis called for help, only to have her cries interrupted by the piercing sound of a gunshot. Hearing her husband groan with pain she jumped out of bed determined to aid him. Grabbing the intruder by the hair Mrs. Davis joined the fight, and as it appeared that the trespasser may be overwhelmed a second shot rang out. Mr. Davis instantly collapsed to the floor with the second shot having struck him in the heart. Unrestrained, the dark figure pushed Mrs. Davis away, dropped his revolver, and ran out of the front door. Realizing that her husband had been badly wounded Mrs. Davis opened the window to scream for help. As she cried out into the night she watched as the man who had murdered her husband walked slowly down the center of S. Burdick St. away from her home.

With an eyewitness to the shooting and a number of pieces of physical evidence including the hat, mask, and murder weapon that the suspect had lost in the Davises' home, Sheriff Shean avidly set about investing the case. After posting notices of a sizable reward for information leading to the murderer's capture, the sheriff brought in any and every man thought suspicious or capable of the crime. At one point there were as many as twenty Davis murder suspects locked up in the county jail at the same time, but after a year of investigation neither sheriff nor seeress was able to locate Mr. Davis's murderer.

Sheriff William S. Downey
Kalamazoo Illustrated.
Frank C. Dayton
and Louis F. Allardt, Chica 1892

CHAPTER 22:
Long a Police Officer
Kalamazoo Gazette, July 4, 1908

I N EARLY MAY 1908, the body of a man was discovered on a train car in Mason, MI. Given the noticeable onset of rigor mortis it was thought that the man had met his fate prior to the train arriving in Mason, with the more likely location of death being the train's original departure point of Kalamazoo. With the murder of Horace Davis fresh in people's minds, and a recent spate of criminal activity attributed to rail yard vagrants, many in Kalamazoo were already on edge. When it was reported that the dead man found in Mason had had his skull crushed and his throat cut, the reaction was tangible. It was under these circumstances that on the morning of May 13th, the once prodigious lawman William S. Downey was found amongst the train cars of the Kalamazoo rail yard. Perhaps remembering previous theories and attempting to settle old scores with the unindicted, William was observed attempting to board and inspect the stationary cars of the yard. When approached by a concerned patrolman, William's behavior was described as erratic, and he was quickly escorted to his home on Village St. After receiving medical attention it was initially reported that with proper rest and recuperation William would soon be on the mend. Sadly, this diagnosis did not prove correct, and in a twist of tragic irony William was admitted to the Michigan Asylum as "insane". Under the care of doctors supervised by Herman Ostrander, who he had once sought for council on the day of the Schilling murder, William S. Downey passed away one month later on the 3rd of July 1908.

William S. Downey lived a life as singular as any man while representing the typical struggles of 19th century Kalamazoo life. He'd begun his life abroad, labored in the soil, and was pressed into the service of his community, during which time he had solidified himself as one of the most prestigious lawmen this community has ever known, and he made rampageous mistakes along the way. It is fitting to remember him in that capacity, as a man aspiring to virtue's side while chasing those who disregarded morality's call. Up until his rapid decline in 1908, William had retained the preponderance of these qualities, as exhibited when barely a year before his confinement to the asylum he garnered one last sensational headline after he undertook what was to be one of his last and surely one of his most spectacular cases.

"Officer Kidnaps Kidnapped Children"
Kalamazoo Gazette, March 3, 1907

East of Kalamazoo, near Delton, a bank operator and former revivalist preacher named Ezra Morehouse lived across the street from his estranged wife. Unsatisfied with the paternal arrangement he found himself in, Ezra concocted a plan to spirit his two young daughters away from their mother. In the execution of this plan he enlisted the assistance of a Grand Rapids "detective" named Shea, Shea's wife, and a young man named Roy Hammond, who was to be the getaway driver. Early one morning, while the former Mrs. Morehouse was giving a music lesson in Hastings, Ezra entered her home and lured his daughters to a waiting touring car. The kidnappers then made a manic break through the countryside in an effort to reach the Michigan/Indiana border. Their getaway was slowed significantly when their vehicle became stuck in some mud, and Ezra was forced to acquire a carriage from a neighboring farm. The kidnappers then trudged onwards towards Indiana much more slowly than they had planned.

It wasn't long before the girls were reported missing, and officers from various local departments and jurisdictions were scouring the countryside. Although ample manpower and resources were engaged in the pursuit of the kidnapped girls, it was not a current member of the force who would acquire the first clue but the inscrutable Detective Downey. Based on a hunch or clue he'd dug up, William boarded the G, R & I and arrived in Sturgis, MI near midnight. Although there was no sign of the missing girls when he arrived, the seasoned lawman's inquiries soon led him to believe that either Lima or La Grange, Indiana was the final destination of the kidnappers. Without resting William continued on and arrived in Lima at 4 o'clock in the morning. There, at the Lima Hotel, William was able to locate Mrs. Shea who had been sent ahead by Ezra to prepare for the girls' arrival. Confident that he had beaten the kidnappers to their destination William lingered at the side of the road near the hotel. Within an hour's time, not long past 5 a.m., a carriage was heard approaching. As Ezra Morehouse, Detective Shea, and their precious cargo entered the ambient light thrown off by the Lima Hotel an imposing figure stepped off of the walk, and there, standing tall in the middle of the road, halted their rig. Like school children rebuked by the headmaster Ezra Morehouse and Detective Shea lost all nerve and relinquished the girls to William. Guiding them to his own carriage William shepherded the girls back across the state line to Sturgis, MI where they boarded a train bound for Kalamazoo. A few hours later, as she waited upon the platform, the girls' anxious mother watched as William exited the train with her daughters in his arms. Crying, she thanked the man who had risen to the task as no other lawman had.

Charles Shean
Sheriff of Kalamazoo 1904-1908.
Pictorial Souvenir of the Police Department and Kalamazoo, Michigan
Wilkinson-Ryan-Haight Co Publishers 1914

Albert Campbell
Sheriff of Kalamazoo 1908-1912.
Kalamazoo Gazette, February 14, 1914

CHAPTER 23:
Brother Betrays Brother

S AID TO HAVE been reared on the milk of human kindness Sheriff Albert Campbell is a notable former citizen of Kalamazoo both in accomplishment and temperament. In 1904, when he lost the election for sheriff to Charles Shean, Albert demonstrated his charitable nature by rallying his backers to the support of the man who had defeated him. When Albert was eventually elected sheriff in 1908, the good will he had previously fostered was put to suitable use. Charles Shean had never given up in his quest to locate Mr. Davis's killer, and together the former and current sheriffs would work diligently together to bring the murderer to justice, with Albert unaware that he would soon be investigating a second much older and equally mysterious unsolved case.

Although the exact bit of detective work that resulted in the clue is unknown, the two industrious Kalamazoo lawmen found themselves traveling to Ionia in February of 1909 to pursue a lead. It was there in the Michigan Reformatory that a man named George Dawson was called from his cell and led to a small room. Once seated, the Kalamazoo officers lobbed question after question regarding the Davis murder at George. Although he initially denied any knowledge of the murder to the officers who interrogated him, the sheer volume of the inquiry soon had George tied up in contradictions. Satisfied that he'd been discovered, George broke down and gave the following account.

On November 24th, 1907, George, his older brother Charles, and a man named Joseph Wallraff found themselves in Grand Rapids. In order to remedy their financial shortcomings the skint trio decided to travel the short distance south to Kalamazoo in order to undertake a series of burglaries. Before doing so George was given the task of cashing a number of forged checks. As he attempted to carry out the ruse as instructed, an observant shopkeeper identified the fraudulent checks and had George arrested. Days later, as the younger Dawson brother sat in prison cursing his bad luck, his older brother Charles arrived for a visit. It was during their ensuing conversation that George found out that his incarceration might not have been the personal misfortune he had believed it to be. Whispering, Charles explained to George that he and Wallraff had arrived in Kalamazoo on the evening of November 25th as planned. After hanging around the rail yard until nearly three in the morning the pair had then set out to find a suitable house to burglarize. They had first looked enviously on the home of E.C. Dayton on S. Burdick, but when they noticed a light on inside coupled with signs of movement, they decided to continue their search. The next home they eyed looked peaceful and inviting, and as Wallraff stood watch near the front door Charles had entered the Davis home. After the robbery had been horribly botched Charles and Wallraff walked a short distance to a pair of stolen bicycles they had stashed. They then rode to a spot near the rail yard and waited for the 5 a.m. train bound for Grand Rapids. When Charles had finished recounting these events to him, George claimed that his brother had bid him farewell, and he had not seen him since.

Charles Dawson c1890.
Kalamazoo Gazette,
February 16, 1909

Joseph Wallraff date unknown.
Kalamazoo Gazette,
August 09, 1914

Although George Dawson would later write a letter to the *Gazette* denying the confession, or that his brother Charles had ever even visited him in prison, the identification of the two suspects was treated as gospel. The significant breakthrough in what many had thought a dying case was met with excitement and high praise in Kalamazoo. In an effort to locate the two suspects implicated by George, Sheriff Campbell flooded the entire continent of North America with postcards describing the wanted men. For months he then did his best to track the alleged murderers, even going so far as to travel to California where Charles Dawson had previously been incarcerated and where his wife was then residing. As many in southwest Michigan anxiously anticipated what seemed imminent news of the capture of the men responsible for Mr. Davis's death, what they instead received was news related to a much older and somewhat forgotten Kalamazoo murder case as it made its way back into the forefront of local consciousness.

For all his collaborative efforts to locate the killer of Horace Davis, it seems that Charles Shean had not been entirely forthcoming regarding developments of another murder case that he had received in 1908 during his last year as sheriff. It transpired that in August of that year, Sheriff Shean had received a cryptic letter from Jackson Prison. Within was a request from Milo Keep asking that the sheriff visit him, whereupon Milo claimed that he would reveal something of significant importance. It was common knowledge that Milo had never given up in his hopes of a successful appeal, and neither had his attorney. In the years preceding Milo's guilty verdict, Attorney Ketcham had worked diligently to secure key witnesses, establish jury misconduct, and form a case implicating W.O. Mclaughlin in the murder of Bert Miller. After Darius Keep passed away at the veteran's home in Grand Rapids in 1906, and Milo had lost his financial support, Attorney Ketcham had even gone so far as to announce his intentions to put up the funds necessary to take Milo's case to the Supreme Court. Likely assuming that Milo wished to discuss one of the ongoing aspects of his appeal with him, Sheriff Shean made his way to Jackson. There, seated across from the rather pitiable convict, the sheriff was caught off guard when Milo leaned forward and presented him with an unexpected question. "If I tell you who the murderer of old man Schilling is, will I get the reward?" Taken aback, Sheriff Shean explained to Milo that it was possible, if his information proved useful, that the reward and sentencing consideration would be forthcoming. Satisfied, Milo went on to explain to Sheriff Shean that the long sought murderer of Louis Schilling was his older brother, William.

The details Milo went on to relay to Sheriff Shean were these: that at about 1 p.m. on the day of the Schilling murder, his brother William had returned to the Keep house, which at that time was in an alley just off Ransom St. between Edwards and Pitcher. Spattered with blood, William buried his clothing in the northwest corner of the woodshed, which was on the east side of the Keep home. William had then borrowed a shirt and pants from Darius and proceeded to stay hidden for two to three days. Three weeks later, Milo claimed, his brother's confidence began to return and William bragged, "You did not think I had nerve enough for a job of that kind, did you?" Milo also claimed that following the murder William was in possession of some cash, when in the days preceding the Schilling murder he had been nearly penniless. Using this money William had purchased a fine rifle, but when he began to fear that it might draw suspicion to him, he traded it off to Milo. Milo claimed that he'd later sold the rifle to local barber Ben Gowen for $3.50 and a watch. According to Milo his brother had later made a more detailed and full confession to him, which included the element that another person had assisted him in the job.

After receiving this unexpected allegation Sheriff Shean returned to Kalamazoo and immediately placed William Keep, who was living in Battle Creek at the time, under surveillance. He then spent the next few weeks attempting to corroborate Milo's story. Although much of what Milo had told him seemed plausible, Sheriff Shean came to believe that William Keep was living in Indiana at the time of the Schilling murder. It had also recently come to light that in 1907, William had bizarrely married Milo's former wife Melissa. Perhaps suspecting the story to have been a lie designed by Milo as an attempt to get back at his brother, and unable to further corroborate his story, Sheriff Shean did not believe that he had evidence enough to proceed with an arrest and left the matter.

It wasn't until August of 1909 as Sheriff Campbell scoured the country for Charles Dawson and Joseph Wallraff that the public finally learned of the revelation conferred to Sheriff Shean the year before. It seems that Milo had been unsatisfied with the steps Sheriff Shean had taken following his disclosure, and he had once again requested the assistance of his attorney. In a detailed statement Milo recounted to Claude Ketchum the tale he had previously told regarding his brother's crime. As he had always been throughout their association, Ketchum was fervent in his willingness to help his client and set out to corroborate Milo's story. Following his own investigation Ketchum claimed that he was unable to find one point of Milo's statement that was provably false. It was confirmed that the Keeps were living in a house in the alley off of Ransom St. in 1893, and the layout of the home and woodshed were just as Milo had described. Information was also reportedly uncovered that indicated that William Keep was living in Kalamazoo during the murder and was even working as a string butcher at the time. More significantly it was soon discovered that this was not the first time that William Keep had been suspicioned as the murderer.

Although there was a large percentage of Kalamazoo that was caught off guard by the revelation that William Keep may have been involved with Louis Schilling's premature death, former Sheriff Wilbur Snow was not among them. It was Wilbur who had arrested the Keeps in 1898 for the attack on Mr. Duggan, and it had been Wilbur who had overseen their incarceration in the county jail during the ensuing trial. It was during this period that Wilbur had intercepted a note written by William and intended for Milo. To the best of his recollection Wilbur claimed that the note read, "If you have given up about this thing, for God's sake keep still about the other," which Wilbur and others assumed was in reference to Milo's knowledge of William's involvement in the Schilling murder. In a sworn statement made out in 1909, Wilbur described the letter and stated that his suspicions regarding William's guilt were such that he had unsuccessfully tried to elicit a confession back in 1898 while the Keeps were under his supervision.

With Milo's story seemingly gaining in credibility it was hoped that charges could be brought against William. Given the specific location provided by Milo regarding where they had been buried, William's bloody clothes were thought the most likely locatable corroborative evidence with which to do this. Unfortunately, while planning for the excavation of the site it was learned that one of the more recent tenants of the previous Keep home had decided to create a cellar and in doing so had dug up the area beneath the woodshed where Milo claimed the bloody clothing had been disposed of. Unable to obtain any physical evidence Sheriff Campbell confronted William Keep in the hopes that he could elicit a confession. Unsurprisingly, William denied any knowledge of the crime and expressed shock that his brother, whom he said he considered innocent of the Bert Miller murder, would point the finger at him. With nothing but Milo's word with which to build a case Sheriff Campbell was forced to return to his more contemporary duties.

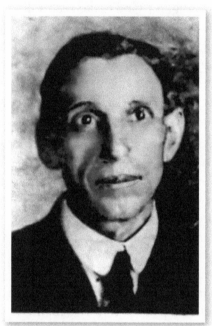

Milo Keep c1920.
Kalamazoo Gazette, December 12, 1920

CHAPTER 24:
Postscript: The Sins of Kalamazoo

Yes, Kalamazoo is a spot on the map
And the passenger trains stop there
And the factory smokestacks smoke
And the grocery stores are open Saturday nights
And the streets are free for citizens who vote
And inhabitants counted in the census
Saturday night is the big night.
Listen with your ears on a Saturday night in Kalamazoo
And say to yourself: I hear America, I hear, what do I hear?

Carl Sandburg

I N DECEMBER OF 1920, Milo Keep returned to Kalamazoo for the first time in fifteen years. As he toured the neighborhoods of downtown where he'd been active as a youth he was astonished at how significantly things had changed. Many of the old businesses he used to know were gone, others had been remodeled, and where shacks used to stand "skyscrapers" of eight to nine stories now rose into the air. Gone were the magnificent carriages and draft animals that used to fill the rutted streets of downtown. In their places were thousands of automobiles that zipped along newly paved roads, which extended in all directions. Within the numerous stores and along every street bustled the citizens of the bourgeoning city that had grown to a robust fifty thousand. And it wasn't just the amount but the people themselves that had changed. Many of those he used to call neighbor had passed or moved on, and of those who remained Milo hoped there were few who remembered him or his previous transgressions.

In truth, a world war, prohibition, and a quickly rebounding economy had laid a blanket of obscurity over many of the crimes of a bygone era. The justice that had once been so fervently sought in cases such as the Schilling and Davis murders was no longer of major concern as the likelihood of solving them and the number of people who once championed such efforts diminished. The majority of the officers who once worked the Schilling case and a large portion of the Schilling family had passed away[5]. Sheriff Albert Campbell, who had so energetically searched the country for the Davis murderer, had also passed on after he was stricken with cancer just one year after leaving office. Had he lived just a few months longer he would have been present when Ralph Chapman came as close as anyone had to obtaining a conviction for one of Kalamazoo's long unsolved murders.

In 1914, Kalamazoo Sheriff Chapman located Joseph Wallraff languishing in a hospital in St. Paul, Minnesota. When approached, Wallraff reportedly shouted, "You don't want me. You want Dawson!" which was partially true. Many would have preferred that the man accused of doing the actual shooting of Mr. Davis had been located, but in his stead the lookout would have to suffice. Wallraff was brought back to Kalamazoo and held in the county jail pending trial. When he arrived, it was noted that Wallraff had become a pitiable addict. The shock of his forced sobriety while incarcerated was so severe that visitation was halted as the fiend fought off the debilitating effects of withdrawal. Although some speculated that he might

---

5 By 1920 Louis Schilling's wife Kate had passed as had four of Louis's eight children, leaving only August, Walter, Clara, and Katherine still living.

not recover, Wallraff did eventually rebound enough to face prosecution. Unfortunately, as they attempted to build their case against him a lack of substantive evidence soon forced Kalamazoo officials to drop the charges. Rather than grant his outright release Wallraff was handed over to officers from Illinois where he was wanted for a parole violation. Wallraff never returned to Kalamazoo or again faced prosecution for his complicity in Mr. Davis's death. Just a half-year after he was transported to Illinois, Wallraff was freed. Returning to St. Paul, and presumably his life of addiction, it was not long before he shot his brother-in-law during a business dispute. As he waited in jail for news of his brother-in-law's death Wallraff somehow got his hands on a revolver. Drawing the weapon, he turned to those present and exclaimed, "I am tired of living," before pressing the revolver to his breast and pulling the trigger.

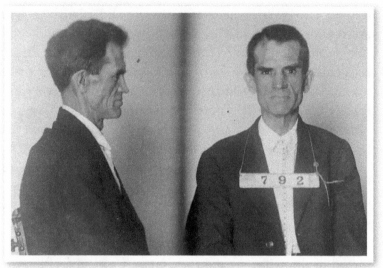

Mugshot of Joseph Wallraff taken in 1914.
Courtesy of The Zhang Collection Center- Western Michigan University

Joseph Wallraff's suicide was in no way the type of closure those in Kalamazoo wanted or ultimately deserved. When the perpetrators of the Davis murder had initially been identified in 1909, many in Kalamazoo were optimistic that justice was imminent. Milo had similarly once offered Kalamazoo a fleeting moment of closure in the Schilling case, but that too faded from grasp. Of those living in Kalamazoo in 1920, Milo was likely the only one who knew the truth regarding the Schilling murder, or maybe he was just the only one who knew if he was lying.

The question of Milo's honesty is an interesting one. He was undisputedly a criminal, but in 1898, he'd not only told the truth regarding the Duggan assault, he'd also testified against his family in court. Credibility is also added to the story he told regarding his brother's involvement in the Schilling murder when you consider the details with which Milo was able to speak about the case fifteen years after it had transpired. As early as 1904, the local papers had made significant mistakes when writing about the Schilling murder. In 1909, Milo seemingly recalled the murder with greater clarity than most in Kalamazoo, even though he was just fifteen at the time it had taken place. There are also lingering doubts concerning his lack of honesty in the Bert Miller murder case. In 1909, just a few months after Milo accused his brother of the Schilling murder, the new wife of W.O. Mclaughlin had come forward with a rather astonishing claim. According to his mistreated wife, W.O. had awoken one night in a fit of remorse and guilt. She claimed that he had then proceeded to confess to killing Bert Miller and seemed overcome by not only the crime but also the idea that Milo was unjustly suffering in prison for it. By 1920, when he was granted an early release from prison, the question of Milo's honesty seemed a somewhat inconsequential matter. He had done the time for the murder of Bert Miller, and William Keep had died in 1912 due to cirrhosis of the liver.

With Kalamazoo moving forward into the twentieth century Milo attempted to do the same. But redemption and the respectable job Milo sought never materialized. Not everyone had forgotten his sordid past, and as he attempted to reintegrate into respectable society his criminal record preceded him. Unable to secure legitimate work Milo was arrested in 1921 when stolen tires were found under his bed in the public house on N. Burdick where he was living. For possession of the stolen property he was once again sent to Jackson Prison, this time for five years.

Looking east down Main towards Portage Street c1927. *From the collection of the Kalamazoo Valley Museum*

The final chapter of Milo Keep's long and gloomy story came in January of 1927 when, during the course of his duties, Patrolman Stevens came across four men who only moments before had cracked a safe in a local store. Somewhat unsurprisingly, the recently freed convict Milo Keep was one of these men. Owing to his long list of previous convictions Milo was now a candidate for prosecution as a habitual offender and his second life sentence. Desperate to avoid such a verdict, he made one last dash for freedom. In the wee morning hours of March 2nd, 1927, Milo worked tirelessly at the west wall of his cell with a spoon until he'd created a hole in the 15-inch brick wall that was large enough to fit through. The 51-year-old criminal then squeezed himself out of his cell and, using a blanket, descended to the ground. For seven months Milo lived what could not have been a comfortable life in hiding. It wasn't until October that Kalamazoo officers followed a known acquaintance of Milo's to a camp of hobos and vagabonds three miles west of the city. There, near a small fire, the officers found the escaped prisoner rolled up in a blanket. Milo was then returned to jail, tried, convicted, and returned to the prison cell where he always seemed destined to be.

There is no satisfying conclusion to be found in the circumstance of Louis Schilling. The distant specter of justice that at times appeared on the horizon would ultimately never materialize. This miscarriage would haunt men like William S. Downey for a lifetime. And yet, for all of the seeming misfortune experienced by those described within this text, the story is one of collective optimism. When faced with such hardship, it was not in our founder's natures to cut short their pursuit of noble ends. Daily we sense the fruits of progress cultivated by these men and women as we pass our institutions of higher learning and smell the smoke leaving the stacks of our bustling factories. Ultimately, those who would take life would not succeed in hindering the pursuit of it. It is now our prerogative as we outwardly nod in muted adulation at the ambitious works of our forebears to allow ourselves just a moment to dwell on the wickedness that often captivates our minds' wondering reflections. For when we look to the hindrances, the impediments, and the characters that live in the grey spaces of history surrounded by scandal and degradation, that is where the nameless murderer can be found. Let us not give the villain more than the passing thought they deserve before returning to the work of Kalamazoo.

CPSIA information can be obtained
at www.ICGtesting.com
Printed in the USA
LVHW110059090822
725446LV00004B/293